Fortune-Telling
with
Playing Cards

Fortune-Telling with Playing Cards

Jonathan Dee

A Sterling / Zambezi Book
Sterling Publishing Co., Inc.
New York

Library of Congress Cataloging-in-Publication Data Available

2 4 6 8 10 9 7 5 3

Published in 2004 by
Sterling Publishing Co., Inc.
387 Park Avenue South
New York, NY 10016

Published and distributed in the UK solely by
Zambezi Publishing Limited
P.O. Box 221 Plymouth,
Devon PL2 2YJ (UK)

Distributed in Canada by Sterling Publishing
c/o Canadian Manda Group
165 Dufferin Street
Toronto, Ontario, Canada M6K 3H6

Distributed in Australia by Capricorn Link (Australia) Pty Ltd.
P.O. Box 704, Windsor, NSW 2756, Australia

Typesetting by Zambezi Publishing, Plymouth UK

Sterling ISBN 1-4027-1219-7
Zambezi ISBN 1-903065-31-3

For information about custom editions, special sales, premium and
corporate purchases, please contact Sterling Special Sales
Department at 800-805-5489 or specialsales@sterlingpub.com.

Contents

1	The Deck of Cards	1
2	Card Groupings for the Poker Deck	21
3	The Aces	26
4	The Twos	32
5	The Threes	37
6	The Fours	42
7	The Fives	47
8	The Sixes	52
9	The Sevens	57
10	The Eights	62
11	The Nines	67
12	The Tens	73
13	The Jacks	78
14	The Queens	83
15	The Kings	88
16	The Joker	93
17	Telling Fortunes the Romany Way	94
18	Romany Card Deck Spreads	110
19	The Lenormand System	124
20	Some Lenormand Spreads	132
21	The Master Method	140
22	The Master Method – Interpretation	161
23	Interpreting The Reading	167
24	Traditional Romantic Games & Readings	178
	Index	181

1

The Deck of Cards

The ordinary deck of playing cards has been used for gaming and fortune-telling for centuries. Fortunes have been won and lost, empires have risen and fallen, and gentlemen have "done the decent thing" and committed suicide (or emigrated) when they could not pay their gambling debts. The turn of a card has been seen as the workings of fate itself, and so profoundly has card-play entered our collective consciousness that many phrases associated with it have entered the language. Everyone who shuffles the deck fervently hopes that:

Luck will be a lady tonight,
What we want is in the cards,
We will play them close to our chests,
We must play the hand that we were dealt,
It is up to us to play our cards right,
We may have an ace up our sleeve,
And we hope that no one else can trump us.

In recent years, fortune-telling with cards has become almost the exclusive province of the Tarot. Not too far back into the past, Tarot cards were hard to come by and the everyday deck of cards with which we are all familiar was a far more accessible tool for foretelling the future.

Playing cards may be the descendants of the Minor Arcana cards of the Tarot, or they may have developed parallel to them.

There is certainly a relationship between the two decks. They both contain four suits. The Hearts, Diamonds, Clubs, and Spades easily translate into their Tarot equivalents of Cups, Coins, Wands, and Swords. In fact, in the latter two suits, Wands are often called Clubs, Staves, or Batons while Spades is a translation of the Italian and Spanish word for Sword.

How to Use This Book

This book falls into three sections. The first two sections require inexpensive playing cards that can be found in almost every household or that can be purchased in any supermarket or small shop around the world. As you will see, the third section is slightly different, but you can still use ordinary playing cards for this section as well.

The first section deals with the normal, everyday 52-card deck that is used in the game of poker and in numerous other card games. I describe the meaning of the cards, together with their individual symbolism, such as the traditional name, the keywords, astrological associations, and the significance of their numbers.

The second and third sections delve into card-reading history and deal with two separate but interrelated strands of interpretation.

The second section is concerned with the Romany Method of card reading; it uses a reduced deck of 32 cards. This system was popularized in France in the latter part of the 18th century by Jean Baptiste Alliette, who is better known by his pen name of Etteilla.

The third section has a totally different slant on the subject of cartomancy. It derives from the work of Mlle Marie Adelaide Lenormand, who read the cards for the Empress Josephine, Napoleon, and many other powerful figures of the day. This system also uses a reduced deck, this time with 36 cards, known as the *"Petit Lenormand."* This deck was developed in the early 19th century. A Lenormand deck shows a beautiful Victorian illustration set into the familiar playing card. If you want to buy a set of these for yourself, you can find them via the Internet. They are produced by a famous card firm called Piatnik, in Vienna. The fact that each card carries an illustration of an ordinary playing card means you can still use this system with a standard playing card deck, unless you decide to treat yourself to a real Lenormand deck.

A series of spreads or card layouts is given at the end of each section. However, as with so much in card reading, the spreads are fluid. So, if you wanted to use the poker deck but fancied trying one of the spreads given in the sections that deal with the Romany Deck or the Lenormand Method, there is nothing to stop you. The secret of successful card reading is experimentation and discovering what works best for you. There are no hard-and -fast rules. In fact, as you gain experience, you will find your own meanings and ways of reading the cards, and these may be completely divorced from anything that has gone before. There are as many ways of reading the cards as there are people who read them. I can guarantee that every single practiced card reader has a unique method of his own. There is no reason why you should be any different.

The Mystery of the Cards

There is a charming fable that probably originates in the early days of card reading in the latter part of the 18th century. The story's setting could be the fabled Atlantis, the faded glory of Ancient Egypt, or Rome as its empire crumbled. Barbarians are at the gates, and the city is about to fall. Within the most holy temple the wise men meet, knowing that all their knowledge and wisdom, their books, their writings will be

> **TIP**
>
> *If you want to use cards for fortune-telling, buy a new deck and break them in by shuffling them a lot. Before using them the first time, ask for help and guidance from your god, spiritual guides, or your higher con-sciousness so that you use the cards well.*
>
> *When you are not using the cards, keep them in their box and within a bag or a box that you keep in a safe place. Never use your fortune-telling deck for card games, and do not allow others to play around with them. Respect your tools and they will respect you – even if the tool in question is a no more than a humble deck of playing cards.*

burned, because these will be worthless as loot to the cruel invaders. In their great wisdom, the aged philosophers agree that their knowledge must be preserved for the ages, but how? The oldest and wisest of the company suggested that since they cannot rely on the highest and most noble aspects of man, they should appeal to his vices. So the deck of cards was created to hide the highest virtue within vice. For as long as man exists, he will want to gamble, little knowing that in that small deck of cards exist many secrets of the past, the future, the nature of existence, and of time itself.

> **NOTE**
>
> *Throughout the book I have tended to use the terms "he" and "him" when referring to the questioner. This is simply to avoid clumsy term-inology—"he or she" and "him / her." As it happens, while card readers may be of either gender, those who wish to consult them are frequently female. No inadvertent sexism is implied.*

Although this story is complete fiction, there is an element of truth about it. Playing cards are complex. They seem to be simple, with their four sets of symbols, numbers from one to ten, a few picture cards, and nothing more, but when one examines them closely, a curious pattern begins to emerge: the pattern is connected to time.

1. There are 52 cards in the deck, equivalent to 52 weeks in the year.
2. The suits are split between black and red, corresponding to day and night.
3. There are four suits, which are equivalent to the four seasons:

Clubs	Spring
Diamonds	Summer
Hearts	Autumn
Spades	Winter

4. There are 13 cards in each suit. Not only are there 13 weeks in each season, there are also 13 lunar months in one year.

Astrologers will also remember that the moon moves 13 degrees in the course of one day.

5.   If the individual numbers of each card in a suit are added, with Aces equaling 1, Jacks, 11, Queens 12 and kings 13, the sum looks like this:

$$1 + 2 + 3 + 4 + 5 + 6 + 7 + 8 + 9 + 10 + 11 + 12 + 13 = 91$$

This is the number of days in a season.

6.   91 x 4 = 364. This is the exact number of days in the fixed lunar year.

Some would argue that the new addition of the Joker makes the calculation complete, bringing the total up to 365. However, this is missing the point; the cards reflect a lunar calendar that was created for an agricultural society. They do not relate to the sophisticated solar system created by the Romans for their urban civilization, which (with minor variations) is the calendar that we use today.

The Devil's Picture Book

As part of the research for this book I came across a website that posed the question, "To play cards is just a fun game—or is it?" It asks, "Isn't card playing in itself harmless if it doesn't become a passion?" The answer is predictable enough: "Whoever is familiar with the origin of playing cards can well understand why such devilish things as fortune-telling are carried on with playing cards."

The article then flatly states that playing cards were invented for the use of the mentally ill King Charles of France in 1392. The designer of the cards was a "degenerate, wicked man who mocked God and His commandments," and for his evil creation he chose Biblical personalities. Continuing the theme, the King represented the devil, the Queen was Mary, the mother of Jesus, while the Jack blasphemously represents Jesus himself. Hearts symbolize the blood of the Lord, while Clubs represent the persecution of the saints (I wonder what happened to Diamonds and Spades?). According to this writer it is not surprising that so much wickedness is associated with gambling and fortune-telling, because the very symbols on the cards are diabolical and were created by a mad, possessed craftsman for an equally mad king. The article ends with another question: "Do you really want to play with the Devil?"

Playing Devil's Advocate

Let's put a few things right! Poor old mad Charles VI of France was indeed in a sorry state when one Jaquemin Gringonneur was commissioned to produce two decks of playing cards for him in 1392, but Charles VI did not invent them. Playing cards had been in existence in Europe for at least twenty years before Gringonneur put brush to parchment. Almost nothing is known of Gringonneur's character, sanity, or beliefs—or indeed of the standard of his work—because none of his cards have survived. The so-called Charles VI deck attributed to Gringonneur that is in the *Bibliotheque National* in Paris has now been proven to be Italian in origin and of a later date.

Equally, there has never been a suggestion that the Queen represented the Virgin Mary or that the King represented the Devil. The role of the Prince of Darkness has traditionally been assigned to the Jack. However, there are Biblical references to be found throughout the entire deck.

Cards Spiritualized

No history of playing cards would be complete without a mention of the ballad "Deck of Cards," which has been performed by many people such as Tex Ritter, Ernest Tubb, and particularly as a country and western song by Wink Martindale in 1959. The song is set during the North African campaign of the Second World War. It concerns an American soldier who is caught with a pack of cards during a church service. The soldier is then hauled before the Provost Marshall and told to explain himself. He does so by explaining the Biblical symbolism of the cards.

The oldest existing version of this ballad dates from 1778 when it was published in Newcastle, England, as a religious tract called "Cards Spiritualized; or, the Soldier's Almanac." The original soldier, Richard Middleton, is Scottish, and the setting is Glasgow. For his apparent blasphemy, Middleton is taken to the mayor, who demands an explanation for his scandalous behavior. Middleton replies that his cards are a Bible, a prayer book, and an almanac, and he goes on to describe each of the cards in turn.

The Ace reminds him that there is one God, and the Deuce of the Old and New Testaments. The Trey is the Father, Son, and Holy Ghost, while the Four is a remembrance of the Four Evangelists, Matthew, Mark, Luke, and John. The Five represents the five wounds of Christ, while the Six symbolizes the days that God took to create heaven and earth. The Seven is the Sabbath when God rested. The Eight are the eight righteous persons saved from the deluge: Noah, his wife, his sons, and his daughters-in-law. The Nine symbolizes the nine lepers cleansed by Christ. The Ten is the Ten Commandments given to Moses. The Queen is the Queen of Sheba, while the King is God himself, and also a reminder to loyally pray for His Majesty King George III. The Knave then became the devil who reported Middleton to the mayor, "The greatest knave that I know."

The "Cards Spiritualized" song also contains a description of the calendar concealed within the deck of cards.

The Origin of Playing Cards

Although it has been claimed that playing cards were invented in China, Korea, or India, no one really knows for certain. Some believe that the cards came to the western world via the Gypsies. However this is unlikely, since the first of the wandering Romany people did not arrive until 1398, and it is known that playing cards were familiar in Europe since at least 1377. A German monk named Johannes of Basel wrote about them in a manuscript, describing them in detail. For the next 20 years various states made laws to prohibit card play among the lower classes.

It seems likely that the cards known in Europe were a fusion of western and Islamic symbolism that had been brought home by returning Crusaders. An ancient deck of 47 cards in the Topkapi Sarayi Museum in Istanbul bears a resemblance to modern playing cards. It has suit symbols similar to those found in the Tarot, with Swords, Cups, Coins, and Polo sticks. Here the similarity ends, because the deck has no picture cards, probably due to a prohibition against the depiction of people in Islamic culture. Apparently, there was no prejudice against gambling with cards in Moslem countries, because the heir to the Turkish throne, Al-Malik Al-Mu'ayyud, was recorded as winning a considerable sum in a card game in 1400 A.D.

European rulers like King Charles VI of France were soon captivated by card games. Following the king's lead, other nobles wanted playing cards of their very own. In 1408 an inventory of the possessions of the Duke and Duchess of Orleans included "one pack of Saracen cards; one card of Lombardy." In the same year comes the very first instance of cards being used to con the public as seen in a court record of two rogues and a game of "Find the Lady"!

It is very likely that playing cards (in their guise as the Minor Arcana of the Tarot) existed before the invention of the Tarot Trumps (the Major Arcana of the Tarot), which was probably created some time between 1420 and 1450 A.D. It is certain that the cheaper, woodblock-printed cards had become the familiar red and black suits by 1448. The suits of Clubs, Diamonds, Spades, and Hearts made their first appearance in France in the same era, and over the succeeding centuries made their way across the world, first to Britain and eventually to the Americas. Other European countries preferred their own variations, Spain and Italy stuck with the Batons, Coins, Swords, and Cups of Tarot tradition, while Germany opted for Bells, Acorns, Leaves, and the familiar Hearts.

The Development of Cartomancy

The origins of card reading go back a very long way, right to the early days of the Roman Empire. An oracle known as the Sybil of Cumae drew prophecies from the random movement of marked leaves on the floor of her cave as they swirled in the draught. However, it took a very long time before our familiar card deck evolved, so fortune-telling with either Tarot cards or playing cards was unknown before the latter part of the 15th century.

The Gypsies may not have introduced playing cards, but they were almost certainly the first to use them for a form of fortune-telling, and they are rightly credited with the swift spread of the practice across continental borders. The first book about using the cards for the purposes of divination appeared in Germany sometime in the 1480s.

By the 1540s French card makers had begun to give the picture cards names and identities, usually of great heroes, kings, and legendary beauties. In the same era, another book on fortune-telling appeared. This volume, by Marcoloni da Forli of Venice, concerned a parlor game played with dice to identify the card that should be interpreted. However, the first custom-made deck, complete with occult imagery for the purposes of divination, did not appear until 1685 in London. Reprinted by John Lenthall in 1712, the deck was advertised as "fortune-telling Cards, pleasantly unfolding the good and bad luck attending human life. With Directions of the Use of the Cards."

Casanova and the Cards

The first ever record of a card reading as we know it occurred relatively recently, historically speaking. In chapter 20 of the monumental *The Story of My Life*, the notorious libertine Giacomo Girolamo Casanova (1725–1798) tells of an episode that occurred in Moscow in 1765. One of his many mistresses, a young Russian peasant girl whom Casanova called Zaira, consulted the cards with unfortunate results. Here is what Casanova wrote about the episode.

"I got home, and, fortunately for myself, escaped the bottle which Zaira flung at my head, and which would infallibly have killed me if it had hit me. She threw herself on the ground, and began to strike it with her forehead. I thought she had gone mad, and wondered whether I had better call for assistance; but she became quiet enough to call me an assassin and a traitor, with all the other abusive epithets that she could remember. To convict me of my crime she showed me twenty-five cards, placed in order, and on them she displayed the various enormities of which I had been guilty."

This discovery of Casanova's many infidelities led to Zaira's deck of cards being thrown on the fire. Understandably, the couple parted the next day.

The Mysterious Etteilla

Five years later, in 1770, the world of card reading changed forever with the publication of *"Etteilla, ou Maniere de se Recreer avec un Jeu de Cardes"* or "Etteilla, Or a Way to Entertain Yourself with a Deck of Cards." The author was Jean Baptiste Alliette (1738–1791) who preferred to reverse his surname to become the mysterious Etteilla. Little is known of his early life, save that he was born in Paris and that he was the son of a cook. His later writings suggest that he had little formal education and that he was most probably self-taught. He married Jeanne Vattier in 1763, but they separated six years later. In his married days, he worked as a seed merchant. Tradition has it that he went on to become a dealer in antique prints and finally a barber and wig maker, although no evidence has ever come to light to confirm this. However, this career change would go a long way toward explaining his popularity as a fortune-teller to aristocratic ladies in an age of such extravagant fashion.

Etteilla later popularized the use of Tarot cards for divination, but in his first book he concentrated on the popular playing card deck—more specifically, a reduced deck of cards with the numbers 2 to 6 removed. Etteilla's reduced deck soon became popular with the Gypsies and thus has been called the Continental or Romany Deck. At no time did Etteilla ever claim that he had invented the system for reading the cards. In fact, he stated that he had learned the art from an unnamed Italian. However, he did invent a new word —cartomancy—to describe the art of reading the cards.

In his book, Etteilla became the first to introduce the concept of reading reversed (upside-down) cards, thereby taking the basic interpretations of the Romany deck from 32 to 64. He later published a deck of playing cards that were commonly known as the *"Petit Etteilla."* In his deck, the pictures or symbols on the cards were within a central border with keywords on all four sides. For example, when the King of Spades was upright, it meant a lawyer, and when reversed, a widower. Likewise the King of Clubs was a country gentleman, and when reversed, a laborer and so on.

Etteilla also has a place in Tarot history, as he was the originator of some of the more outlandish theories concerning the origins and true meanings of the cards. Details of this aspect of his career can be found in my book *Tarot Mysteries*.

It could be said that after enjoying a considerable vogue in the France of Louis XVI and Marie Antoinette, history finally caught up with Etteilla with the coming of the French Revolution in 1789. Etteilla died in 1791 just after the publication of his playing cards.

The turbulent revolutionary fervor swept away the genteel, bewigged world of Etteilla, but the stage was set for the appearance of another extraordinary character, one who was to have a profound influence on both the direction of card reading and possibly of the world itself—this was Mlle. Marie Adelaide Lenormand.

Madamoiselle de Lenormand

One of the most extraordinary figures in the history of card reading was Marie Ann Adelaide de Lenormand, latterly known as the Sibyl of the Faubourg St. Germain. Born on May 5, 1772, she was the daughter of a wealthy cloth merchant of Alencon, France, and she was one of three children. Always a difficult child, Marie became the bane of her respectable father's life. He confined his rebellious daughter to a convent and then tried to forget all about her. Fate then played a card that ended both Marie's father's life and lost the family fortune in one stroke. No longer able to afford to eat, let alone pay her school fees, at the age of fourteen Marie found herself working as a laundress alongside a certain Madame Gilbert. Madame Gilbert was considered an expert fortune-teller, so under her maternal tutelage, young Marie became adept at the arts of palmistry, numerology, and the one that would eventually make her famous— cartomancy.

The next episode of Marie's life remains something of a mystery. It is said that she spent her fifteenth year in London studying all manner of mystic arts, such as astrology and the Qabalah, although how a penniless young laundress could have managed this is open to speculation.

Marie was certainly in Paris at the onset of the French Revolution in 1789, a fact that brings us back into the realms of the known. It is said that in times of uncertainty and fear, those who can provide a glimpse of what is to come will always do very well, and Marie prospered when many others did not. Her clientele grew to include some of the most notable revolutionaries, such as Danton, Desmoulins, Marat, Saint Just, and even the "incorruptible" Maximilian Robespierre himself. Of course this was not without its risks. Most of her prominent clients met their ends beneath the blade of the guillotine, although Marat was knifed while having a bath. Indeed, most were sent to their deaths by a stroke of the implacable Robespierre's pen. The risk to Marie was multiplied when she rashly told Robespierre that he would go the same way within a year. This prediction was to cost Marie her freedom and ensure her a place in history.

During her confinement, Marie made the acquaintance of a young aristocratic widow from the French colony of Martinique who, like Marie, was destined for the guillotine, her husband having been beheaded some time previously. The lady's name was Josephine Beauharnais. The two became firm friends. Josephine had always been fascinated by divination and had some knowledge of the voodoo that was practiced in her native island. She was equally fascinated by the attitude of Marie Lenormand, who seemed unperturbed by the threat of death that hung over them both. As it turned out, Marie's prediction to Robespierre soon came true, and he followed so many of his victims to the blade. With his execution, the Terror ended and the two women were freed.

The next episode of French history is called the *Directoire*. This was a time when the revolution entered a calmer phase. Josephine, always the social climber, rapidly became the mistress of the chief of state. In the process, she met her future husband, a young Corsican general named Napoleone Buonaparte. With the increasing influence of her friend Josephine, Marie Lenormand's reputation grew. She was introduced into the upper echelons of post-revolutionary society, many of whom wanted to employ her services. During the Napoleonic consulate and the empire that followed, Marie accurately read the cards for such worthies as Marshall Bernadotte, predicting that he would become a king. He did—and he founded the ruling dynasty of Sweden.

Eventually, Marie's close association with the Empress Josephine was to cause her second period of imprisonment. In 1809, Napoleon (now spelling his name in the French manner) decided that Josephine was too old to give him the heir that he craved. He now wanted a younger, better-connected princess to be the mother of his future dynasty. He secretly entered negotiations with Austria for the hand of the Arch-Duchess Marie Louise. These events were clearly seen in the cards by Lenormand, who told Josephine of the impending divorce. Napoleon was so angry that he had Marie imprisoned until the deed had been done. At least, that is the official version. According to Lenormand herself, she confronted Bonaparte with her knowledge, but he met her furious outburst with one of his own, and the outraged seeress threw a deck of cards in the emperor's face. Either way, Marie Lenormand ended up doing time again!

The occupation of Paris by the allied forces of Britain, Russia, and Prussia in 1814 did nothing to harm Lenormand's reputation. Indeed, she was consulted by no less a figure than the Tsar Alexander I, who immediately recommended her services to the Duke of Wellington.

Shortly after this, Marie considered it prudent to remove herself to Brussels, taking advantage of the invitation of the Prince of Orange (she accurately predicted that he would become king of the newly founded kingdom of Holland). However her luck then ran out. She was arrested for cheating the customs and was again imprisoned.

On her eventual return to Paris, Marie established a salon where she continued to read the fortunes of high society, becoming known as the Sibyl of the Faubourg St Germain. However, her glory days were past, and by the time of her death in 1843, she had quietly slipped into obscurity.

Marie's great-niece, Mlle. Camille le Normand (she had altered the spelling slightly) published a book called *Fortune-Telling by Cards* outlining her relative's methods. Over the next 150 years or so, many versions of her symbolic personal deck were published, usually entitled "Lenormand Fortune Cards," often with an extremely misleading blurb which went something like this:

"In the early years of the nineteenth century, there was a powerful gypsy fortune-teller who predicted the victories of Napoleon as well as his eventual defeat. The secrets of this gypsy witch are now yours."

The fact that Marie Ann Adelaide Lenormand was neither a witch nor a gypsy made no difference whatsoever to the card manufacturers.

Typical Lenormand Cards

Although cards of this type can still be purchased reasonably cheaply today, often with a little poem explaining the card's meaning inset into the design, it is not strictly necessary to have a fully illustrated deck of cards to read in the Lenormand way. After all, the great lady herself was content with an ordinary deck of 36 cards (exactly the same number as is used in the ancient card game of Piquet which was extremely popular in Lenormand's day).

It is certain that the process popularized by Etteilla and Lenormand found its way into middle-class parlors around the world. Card oracles as a game or pastime became very popular throughout the 19th century, and they received another boost with the vogue for Spiritualism in the 1850s. This new movement gave everything with an esoteric flavor an added excitement and led the way to the occult revival of the latter part of the century.

The Star-Craft of the Golden Dawn

The grandly named Hermetic Order of the Golden Dawn was a very well-heeled, upper-class offshoot of the Masonic Order that was established in 1887. Its founding fathers, Dr. William Wynn Wescott (1848–1925), Dr. Robert Woodman (1828–1925) and Samuel Mathers (1854–1918) were convinced that they had found many of the secrets of the universe by the study of ancient occult lore. The Tarot deck in particular was an object of fascination to the members who considered each card to be a key that would unlock cosmic truths. Consequently, a great deal of effort was made to both come up with a system to tie in the 22 pictorial cards of the Major Arcana with the Hebrew Qabalah, numerology, and astrology. After this monumental exercise was completed, the order turned its attention to the Minor Arcana with its suits of Clubs (now renamed Wands), Coins (now renamed Pentacles), Swords, and Cups. These now received an astrological treatment, with planets and signs allocated to each of the pip cards, while whole star signs were granted to the courts (the details can be found in my book *Tarot Mysteries*).

The final outcome of this was a coherent system of astrological attributions for the Minor Arcana of the Tarot. There is a small problem in that there are 12 signs of the zodiac, each representing a character type, while the Tarot has four court cards per suit, making 16 in all, rather than the more usual three court cards in a playing card deck. The upshot of this was that the Pages, the equivalents of the Jacks, fell out of the system, giving the Tarot a rather awkward correspondence to traditional astrology. On the other hand, the system devised by Mathers does fit a standard playing card deck rather well, although it is unlikely that this fact ever occurred to him.

In this system of attributions, the first point to bear in mind is the association of the suits to the four traditional elements of Fire, Water, Air, and Earth. Clubs are identified with Fire, Hearts to Water, Spades to Air, and Diamonds to Earth.

As we all know, the zodiac consists of twelve signs, namely Aries the Ram, Taurus the Bull, Gemini the Twins, Cancer the Crab, Leo the Lion, Virgo the Maiden, Libra the Scales, Scorpio the Scorpion, Sagittarius the Archer, Capricorn the Goat, Aquarius the Water-Carrier, and Pisces the Fish. These signs are subdivided among the four classical elements so that Aries is a Fire sign, Taurus is governed by Earth, Gemini by Air, Cancer by Water, and so on, in a never-ending sequence.

The Golden Dawn did not consider the signs of this familiar form of astrology to be the oldest type of zodiac in existence. The

FIRE	EARTH	AIR	WATER
(CLUBS)	*(DIAMONDS)*	*(SPADES)*	*(HEARTS)*
Aries	Taurus	Gemini	Cancer
Leo	Virgo	Libra	Scorpio
Sagittarius	Capricorn	Aquarius	Pisces

members of the mystical order were enamored of the magic and mystery of Ancient Egypt, so they also adopted the system of Decans from the civilization of the Nile. To put it simply, a decan consists of ten degrees (a sign of the zodiac being thirty degrees, or one twelfth of a circle). So each sign of the zodiac is made up of three decans, making thirty-six decans in all. All that remained was to find the right card for the right decan.

The first step in this process was to remove the Aces from each suit, because it was considered that they represented the purest or archetypal forms of their respective elements. Thus the Ace of Clubs was given the esoteric title of "The Root of the Powers of Fire"; likewise, the Ace of Hearts was considered to be "The Root of the Powers of Water," and so on. It is for this reason that the Aces do not appear in the zodiac arrangement of the minor cards, but are represented by all three signs of their respective elements. Hence the Ace of Clubs is associated with the three Fire signs of Aries, Leo, and Sagittarius. The Ace of Hearts is allocated the Water signs of Cancer, Scorpio, and Pisces, the Ace of Spades gains the attributions of the Air signs of Gemini, Libra, and Aquarius while the Ace of Diamonds connects with the Earth signs of Taurus, Virgo, and Capricorn.

The twelve picture cards, Jack, Queen, and King did not quite fit the scheme either, so these too were removed from this system and granted a star sign each.

With the Aces and court cards now removed, we are left with thirty-six numbered cards, providing a perfect fit for the thirty-six decans. After a fierce dispute, the Two of Clubs became associated

CLUBS	SPADES	HEARTS	DIAMONDS
(FIRE)	*(EARTH)*	*(AIR)*	*(WATER)*
KING	KING	KING	KING
Aries	*Capricorn*	*Libra*	*Cancer*
QUEEN	QUEEN	QUEEN	QUEEN
Leo	*Taurus*	*Aquarius*	*Scorpio*
JACK	JACK	JACK	JACK
Sagittarius	*Virgo*	*Gemini*	*Pisces*

with the first decan of Aries. The Three was identified with the second decan, and the Four with the third, all being found within the element of Fire. For the Five, Six, and Seven of Clubs, the three decans of the next Fire sign, Leo were used. Finally the Eight, Nine, and Ten were given the three decans of Sagittarius. The same formula was followed for all the remaining minor cards.

Now the problem became how to individualize the cards so that they arrived at a coherent divinatory meaning. To address this problem, Mathers proposed a sequence of the seven astrological planets in the following order: Mars, the Sun, Venus, Mercury, the Moon, Saturn, and finally, Jupiter. This particular order of the planets is based on a medieval system known as the planetary hours, which in its original form was used to help magicians and those involved in witchcraft to invoke suitable powers for their spells. Be that as it may, the order of the planets was then combined with the decan system to provide an individual meaning for each card. The following table clearly shows the system.

Now, each numbered card contained the symbolism of a number, an element, a planet and a sign of the zodiac; the Aces were considered separately. This is fertile ground to establish the modern meanings of the individual cards.

Of course, the Golden Dawn system of card attribution is not set in stone. Many card readers have developed their own methods and most probably ignore these astrological attributions. Nevertheless, for the sake of completeness, the Golden Dawn astrological attributions are included in the sections describing the individual cards.

The Cards of the Poker Deck

The following pages give the meanings of each of the 52 cards in the standard deck. They are arranged by their respective numbers or names, together with their significance in terms of numerology, their astrological correspondence according to the Golden Dawn, and their traditional nicknames or relevant keywords. In addition, the curious symbolism of Mlle. Lenormand is mentioned, together with her equally unique numbering system. More details of this can be found in the third part of the book.

In the case of the court cards, there is also a description of their traditional appearance and of the legendary or historical characters each is supposed to represent. In most cases, these identities are French in origin and they were assigned to the cards in the middle of the 16th century.

Each card is preceded by a four-line verse dating from the 19th century as part of a fortune-telling parlor game, in which the cards

CARD	PLANET	ZODIAC SIGN	DECAN
2 Clubs	Mars	Aries	1
3 Clubs	Sun	Aries	2
4 Clubs	Venus	Aries	3
5 Diamonds	Mercury	Taurus	1
6 Diamonds	Moon	Taurus	2
7 Diamonds	Saturn	Taurus	3
8 Spades	Jupiter	Gemini	1
9 Spades	Mars	Gemini	2
10 Spades	Sun	Gemini	3
2 Hearts	Venus	Cancer	1
3 Hearts	Mercury	Cancer	2
4 Hearts	Moon	Cancer	3
5 Clubs	Saturn	Leo	1
6 Clubs	Jupiter	Leo	2
7 Clubs	Mars	Leo	3
8 Diamonds	Sun	Virgo	1
9 Diamonds	Venus	Virgo	2
10 Diamonds	Mercury	Virgo	3
2 Spades	Moon	Libra	1
3 Spades	Saturn	Libra	2
4 Spades	Jupiter	Libra	3
5 Hearts	Mars	Scorpio	1
6 Hearts	Sun	Scorpio	2
7 Hearts	Venus	Scorpio	3
8 Clubs	Mercury	Sagittarius	1
9 Clubs	Moon	Sagittarius	2
10 Clubs	Saturn	Sagittarius	3
2 Diamonds	Jupiter	Capricorn	1
3 Diamonds	Mars	Capricorn	2
4 Diamonds	Sun	Capricorn	3
5 Spades	Venus	Aquarius	1
6 Spades	Mercury	Aquarius	2
7 Spades	Moon	Aquarius	3
8 Hearts	Saturn	Pisces	1
9 Hearts	Jupiter	Pisces	2
10 Hearts	Mars	Pisces	3

were shuffled and laid out face downward on a tabletop. Each person would then close his or her eyes and choose a single card. The verse was then read out for the amusement of all who were assembled. For more games of this sort see the chapter on "Traditional Romantic Games and Readings" in this book.

2

Card Groupings for the Poker Deck

The Color of the Reading

The most obvious and inescapable feature of any reading is the color of the cards. A predominance of the red cards (Hearts and Diamonds) is an indicator that the reading is generally positive and that the outcome of any question will be a happy one. The reverse is true if the predominant color is black (Clubs and Spades). The result of a reading with a preponderance of these cards is more troublesome and worrying.

The Suits

If one suit is predominant in a spread, this will reveal the main sector of life concerning the questioner.

Clubs

If Clubs make up the majority of the cards in a spread, there are new opportunities coming up as well as encounters with new people. Friendships and the influence of people around the questioner become very important. However, there is a danger that the questioner will be too optimistic for his own good and that he will take on far more than he can comfortably handle.

Diamonds

A majority of Diamonds in a reading indicates the importance of business matters and financial dealings. If Diamonds totally dominate the reading, then there is the danger that the questioner is too materialistic, and that he is consumed by thoughts of profit. On the other hand, there is also an indication of monetary worries.

Spades

This difficult suit has a troublesome reputation, so if the Spades overwhelm a spread then hard times are indicated. The suit tells of confusion, anxiety, and it may even warn of physical danger. Impress upon your questioner that a positive mental attitude will be needed to sustain him through these problems.

Hearts

The suit of Hearts is considered a good omen, so a prevalence of these in a spread cannot fail to be an excellent indicator of joyful times ahead. On the other hand, too many Hearts may denote a person who is self-indulgent, pleasure seeking, and inconsiderate toward others.

Card Values

If most of the cards in the reading are numbered Seven or above (this includes picture cards and Aces), it is a sign that major moves are afoot in the questioner's life. It indicates that fate has taken a hand in the questioner's affairs and that the changes that are about to occur will be very important.

Low cards, Twos to Sixes, show that the questioner's life will continue to follow the same general pattern with the same habits, activities, and concerns continuing. It may be an indication that the questioner is basically happy about this familiar existence and that he is not ready to take on the challenges of major change.

Card Combinations

A combination of cards in a spread takes on extra significance. Although the Twos do not have a special meaning, a pair may be taken to indicate a particular numerological significance. For instance, two Sixes would lead one to consider the meaning of the number 6. Details of each numerological interpretation are given in the individual card interpretation sections.

The combination meanings given below are suitable for the full Poker Deck. Card combinations used with the reduced Romany Deck are given in the relevant chapter.

Four Aces
A very good indicator of success in all areas of life.

Three Aces
Enthusiasm and energy, new opportunities and self-confidence.

Four Twos
Oversensitivity, a hint of guilt, and a need to be discreet.

Three Twos
Happy times spent in the company of loved ones where one can talk openly and deeply and share thoughts and ideas.

Four Threes
It is not wise to listen to gossip or believe everything that you hear.

Three Threes
Lots of new information. This could be an indication of education in the widest sense, academic study, or of a more personal revelation.

Four Fours
Plan carefully and work out the next move. It may signal a departure from anything that has been previously attempted.

Three Fours
Overcoming an obstacle to progress. The questioner will have the opportunity to rest and recuperate before new challenges are undertaken.

Four Fives
An indicator of many choices. Difficult decisions have to be made.

Three Fives
A need to escape from difficult circumstances. This may show a rising sense of panic that could lead to unwise actions. A cool head would be a great advantage at this time.

Four Sixes
A restful period, which is a pleasant respite even though it does not advance the questioner's practical interests.

Three Sixes

Friends and colleagues will provide the questioner with a new opportunity.

Four Sevens

An indicator of solitude and feelings of isolation. This introspective period will help clarify many issues.

Three Sevens

The questioner should ignore other people's opinions and hold to his course even though there are temporary problems.

Four Eights

Temporary financial and business worries.

Three Eights

An improvement in monetary prospects. The questioner will do something positive to ease the financial burden.

Four Nines

This is an excellent indicator of luck, although it would be best to be humble, as others will tend to resent the questioner's success.

Three Nines

An unexpected accolade or a change of attitude for the better. This may apply to those around the questioner who have been critical in the past.

Four Tens

The end of an era—but this is all to the good. This combination indicates a clean slate and the start of a new, exciting project.

Three Tens

Improvements in finances. This could bring a windfall to some or the final repayment of a loan for others.

Four Jacks

Disputes and quarrels among immature people.

Three Jacks

The questioner needs to calm down a heated situation.

Four Queens

For a man, four Queens show that he may be embarrassed or compromised by his associates. For a woman, there will be backstabbing and spite among female acquaintances.

Three Queens
New female friends who will prove influential in the future.
Four Kings
For a man, high achievement, added responsibilities, and the respect and admiration of others. For a woman, it is not good, as it suggests jealousy within a relationship and conflict between men.
Three Kings
This is a good combination for both men and women. For a man it denotes true friendship and the help and support of his peers. For a woman, three Kings shows the possibility of romance and an enjoyable social life.

Adjacent Cards

It is a general rule that more information about a card's meaning will come from the suit of the card that immediately precedes it in a spread. However, should any card be flanked by two cards of the same suit, then it is likely that its meaning will be changed in some way because it will take on some of the traits of the surrounding suit. For instance, when a particularly troubling card like the Nine of Spades—which means worries, sleepless and nights and mental anguish—is flanked by two Hearts, the likelihood is that there is an emotional cause to this problem and that it will soon be relieved. If the dreadful Nine of Spades were to be flanked by two Clubs, then the questioner could call upon and receive the help and support of friends. It if were surrounded by Diamonds, then an injection of money would alleviate the problem. Conversely, should a Heart such as the Two (a card of love and attraction) be flanked by two Spades, the time lovers spend together is likely to be unpleasant and quarrelsome.

3

The Aces

Aces represent the number one. Quite apart from the significance of numbering in card reading, each number has symbolic associations of its own. The number one is likened to the rising sun: it is an initiator, and it obviously relates to new beginnings. As a concept, the number one is masculine, phallic, and active. It shows readiness to start something, to forge ahead and to get things moving. If Aces are prominent in your reading, something totally new is about to happen, and you are about to enter unknown and exciting territory.

Each of the four Aces corresponds to one of the four elements of Fire, Earth, Air, and Water, according to its suit. Therefore, Clubs relate to the fiery element of creativity, new enterprise, and impulse. Diamonds correspond to the fruitful earth, practicality, common sense, and material values. Spades are associated with the air and the intellect; they can be as gentle as a breeze or as destructive as a tempest. The emotional suit of Hearts is symbolically connected to the element of water, to intuition and feelings, to those who are shallow, and to those who are very deep indeed.

There is no escaping it; the Ace of Spades has a very bad reputation indeed. Many people consider it to be the "death card," the equivalent of the dreaded number 13 in the Tarot deck. This belief was so prevalent that, during the Vietnam War, American commandos left the Ace of Spades behind them as a sinister "calling card" as part of their psychological warfare campaign after raiding Vietcong positions. In addition, in many decks the Ace of Spades often possesses a more elaborate design than the other three. This is because this was once the "duty Ace," which was the printed proof that tax had been paid to the British Crown on the pack of cards. This tax dated from 1588 and was finally abolished in 1960 because collecting it was more trouble than it was worth. So, the Ace of Spades is the cardboard embodiment of the old saying "There are only two certainties in this world—death and taxes!"

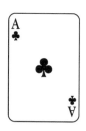

The Ace of Clubs

"He that doth draw the Ace of Clubs,
From his wife gets a thousand snubs;
But if maids do it obtain,
It means that they shall rule and reign."

Keywords: Success, action, initiative, creativity.

Astrological Relationship: The element of Fire. Since the Ace of Clubs is the first card in the playing-card sequence, it is apt that it belongs to the element of Fire, which is the primal furnace from which everything was born. The Ace represents the spark of life, the essence or soul. It symbolizes the urge to come into being. This is tentative at first, but just as a tiny flame can become a great conflagration or a feeble shoot eventually develops into a mighty tree, the potential contained within the symbolism of the Ace of Clubs is awesome.

Meaning: The Ace of Clubs is an excellent card, because it signifies a burst of energy, a new beginning, and enormous potential. The card is connected to the expression of talent and a capacity for original thinking.

The Ace of Clubs can indicate either a financial gain, fame, or public recognition for an achievement. In short, this Ace means good news—probably concerning money, but it may also signify an improvement in personal status as a reward for past efforts.

If the Ace of Clubs is found among the first three cards in a spread, it is a sign of extraordinary talent. The questioner is in possession of unique gifts that can take him a long way if he channels them in a productive fashion.

Lenormand Number and Symbol: 25; Ring.

The Ace of Diamonds

"Since that this Ace is now your lot,
You will wed one that's fierce and hot;
But if a woman does draw it,
She will wed one with wealth and wit."

Keywords: Money, luck, communication.

Astrological Relationship: The element of Earth. Practicalities and a solid day-to-day routine provide the necessary structure that underpins our more exciting activities. Earth is fruitful and bountiful. It is the source of wealth, both in terms of nature and the precious minerals that are found deep below the surface. It takes hard work and persistence to persuade the earthy element to give up its riches, and this is the lesson of the Ace of Diamonds.

Meaning: The traditional meaning of this card is a message—possibly in the form of a letter. In this age of instantaneous communication I see no reason why the Ace of Diamonds should not represent a phone call, text message, or e-mail.

In keeping with the earthy and generally materialistic nature of the Diamond suit, the message the Ace brings is usually connected with money. This is a positive card, so the news is likely to be profitable to the questioner. One of this Ace's subsidiary meanings is a successful exam result.

The card is also associated with marriage, or at least with the establishment of a long-term partnership. In a traditional reading, the Ace of Diamonds signifies a marriage proposal made to a female questioner, but to a male it indicates a business proposition that will turn a remarkable profit.

If the Ace of Diamonds is among the first three cards in a spread, it signifies an opportunity for the questioner to use his abilities in a practical way that will enhance his reputation and his bank balance.

Lenormand Number and Symbol: 31; Sun.

The Ace of Spades

"Thou that dost draw the Ace of Spades,
Shall be sore flouted by the maids;
And when it is a damsel's lot,
Both love and honor go to pot."

Keywords: Endings, death, challenges, ruthlessness.

Astrological Relationship: The element of Air. As changeable as the wind, the Ace of Spades blows away the cobwebs to allow you to see the truth. This is not always a pleasant experience, but it is an enlightening one. Air is symbolically connected with physical and mental strife as well as verbal and intellectual challenges.

Meaning: The Ace of Spades shows that this is the time to ditch the past and make a fresh start, to solve existing problems and resolve old enmities. Only when this uncomfortable process has been completed can one move on to a new phase of life. Illusion is banished by the appearance of the Ace of Spades. Cozy, comforting dreams are swept away by the harsh wind of pitiless reality that cuts like a blade through one's most cherished fantasies.

This Ace signifies great power. The wind of change is blowing and it cannot be resisted. It acts like a clarion call to accomplish great things. How this is to be done needs careful consideration.

Although this Ace is called "the death card," rarely, if ever, does it actually signify the death of a person. However, it does indicate the death of an idea, so it forces one to discard whatever is outworn and useless in one's life. This can be a ruthless process that forces understanding and clarity upon the mind. This is likely to be an unwelcome development.

If found among the first three cards in a reading, the Ace of Spades shows that the questioner has leadership ability and that he can influence others in a profound way.

Lenormand Number and Symbol: 29; Lady.

The Ace of Hearts

"He that draws the Ace of Hearts
Shall surely be a man of parts;
And she that draws it, I profess,
Will have the gift of idleness."

Keywords: Home, family, love, passion, creativity.

Astrological Relationship: The element of Water. This is the element of the emotions. It is said that still waters run deep, and this is very evident in the Ace of Hearts. In addition to presiding over love, the card also hints at creativity, artistry, music, mysticism, and the ebb and flow of emotions of all kinds.

Meaning: The Ace of Hearts is traditionally known as the "home card," and it is connected to those whom we love. The appearance of this Ace often indicates good news coming from or to a family member or close friend. It may signal the return of a prodigal relation or one who has been out of contact for some time. The Ace of Hearts may also show the ending of a dispute and a readiness to forgive and forget.

The Ace of Hearts may show the establishment of a home with a partner and is therefore indicative of marriage. In a more general sense, the Ace of Hearts shows happiness and a congenial atmosphere that is shared with special people. One aspect that is impossible to ignore is its association with passion and romance. So, the card could easily indicate the commencement of a new, exciting love affair, especially if the questioner is young. On the other hand, the enthusiasm indicated by this card may be as easily directed toward a new hobby or a creative enterprise.

If the Ace of Hearts is one of the first three cards, it shows that the questioner is very emotional with deep affections and loyalties.

Lenormand Number and Symbol: 28; Man.

4

The Twos

Two is the number of duality. It is considered feminine, passive, and receptive. Symbolically, the number is related to the New Moon for it is at this time that both Sun and Moon are in conjunction. In card reading, Twos often indicate a need to learn patience. They could signal the first tentative steps in a new love affair. A predominance of Twos can indicate a meeting of minds or hearts or conversely, the confusion caused by two totally incompatible points of view.

The Two of Clubs

"Note that this deuce doth signify
That thou a loyalist shalt die;
The damsels that the same shall take
Never will their good friends forsake."

Keywords: Potential, support, opportunity.

Astrological Relationship: Mars in Aries. Mars is powerfully placed its own sign of the Ram. It is energetic, forceful, assertive, dominant, and bold. This is an extremely masculine force, and is an excellent sign for getting things up and running, but can also show negative features such as impatience, irritability, and a desire for confrontation.

Meaning: In essence the Two of Clubs is a card of potential. Opportunities and invitations are on their way. These may seem to be initially unimportant, but this is a time of promise. The pressure is on when the Two of Clubs is present. It means that the questioner should be more self-reliant than he has been. It is likely that he feels that he has bitten off more than he can chew and will count on his friends and family to support him through a difficult period.

However, it is vital that this cry for help is not taken too far, because this could dearly cost close relationships. These are likely to suffer under the strain, so the questioner may find that those who were constantly around him have become more distant. If ever there was a time for wisdom this is it! It's time to abandon unrealistic expectations and to bring things back to basics, to avoid leaning so heavily on the goodwill of loved ones, and to budget wisely for the future.

The Two of Diamonds

"Hast thou not drawn the number two?
Thy spouse shall be both just and true.
But if a woman this now have,
Beware a sly and crafty knave!"

Keywords: Unexpected news and money.

Astrological Relationship: Jupiter in Capricorn. The optimism of Jupiter is combined with the innate shrewdness of the sign of the Mountain Goat, indicating tremendous resourcefulness and the ability to take on daunting tasks. There may be a tendency to concentrate on details while ignoring larger issues.

Meaning: This is a card of good news, and because it is a Diamond, the glad tidings are likely to involve finances, investments, and windfalls. The amount may not be overly large, but it will be welcome. If good news concerning money is on offer then this is likely to come from someone close to the questioner rather than from some official source. It may be that a close friend or relative is the actual recipient of the cash, but even if this is the case, the questioner's pal will not forget him, so he will benefit indirectly.

Regarding indirect benefits: the Two of Diamonds could be seen symbolically as a karmic benefit, a reward for past efforts the questioner has made on behalf of others.

In a question of love, this Two can show a happy, fulfilling love affair, but one that meets with disapproval and suspicion from outsiders.

The Two of Spades

"Always this deuce betokens strife,
And with a scolding, wicked wife;
But if a woman's lot it be,
Honor, great love, and dignity."

Keywords: Pause, tact, cautious optimism.

Astrological Relationship: The Moon in Libra. The emotionally charged Moon gains a little balance and stability in the sign of the Scales. This suggests a delicate balance between two equal forces. This card may point to a time of harmony, but it could imply difficulty in arriving at a decision.

Meaning: As Spades go, this is not a bad card. The Two indicates a delicate situation, one in which the questioner feels as if he is walking on eggshells and avoiding saying the wrong thing. Problems shown by this card are temporary, and it may be that all the questioner has to do is to wait until the dust has settled and tempers around him are not so frayed. Even so, there is room for movement. The questioner may be cautiously diplomatic, and he may act as a tactful go-between, smoothing out ruffled feelings so that peace gets a chance.

Although this is a situation that no one would want to be in, the way is which the questioner deals with it will enhance his reputation and lead on to the next cycle of his life, one that is more promising than the one that has gone before.

The Two of Hearts

"He who can draw the deuce shall be
Endowed with generosity;
But when a woman draws the card,
It doth betide her cruel hard."

Keywords: Happiness, contentment, simple pleasures.

Astrological Relationship: Venus in Cancer. The planet of love in the clannish sign of the Crab indicates a particularly strong emotional bond with those who offer security and support. A love of home comforts and familiar people is emphasized. It may also show that instincts are particularly strong at this time and that personal insights will border on psychic awareness.

Meaning: In older traditions, the Two of Hearts can mean the commencement of love, a happy marriage, and love letters. However, there are several other cards in the Hearts suit that effectively mean the same thing. In this case, we are looking not so much at the excitement and passion of new love but at a feeling of contentment, and a quieter, less lively aspect of the emotional self. Therefore, the card can mean the small things that make the questioner's life worth living. This could indeed relate to a particular love affair, in which case it represents quiet moments spent with a loved one.

It could just as easily refer to the pleasure a person gets when puttering about in the garden, enjoying a particularly beautiful view, listening to inspiring music, or playing with a beloved pet. These moments are often forgotten in the bustle of life. The Two of Hearts reminds us to appreciate them, to stop and smell the flowers, and to gain strength from the joy of simple things.

5

The Threes

Three is an extremely creative number that is symbolically connected to the expansive, exuberant optimism of the planet Jupiter. Therefore, the Three is about broadening horizons and moving past previously established boundaries. The influence of this optimistic number can lead one to be unrealistic, which brings us to the downside of the number Three. When reality bites, it can shake the self-image considerably, leading to a rapid reassessment and a desire to cut one's losses. On the other hand, this will work toward the good in the long run, because Jupiter often knocks something down in order to replace it with something better and brighter. This number opens the door to new experiences.

The Three of Clubs

"You by chance this trey have drawn,
Shall on a worthless woman fawn.
A maiden that shall draw this trey
Shall be a lass that ne'er says nay."

Keywords: Feud or forgiveness

Astrological Relationship: The Sun in Aries. The Sun is the most powerful force in astrology, but when it is found in Aries it achieves an exceptional intensity and is considered to be "exalted" in the sign of the Ram. One major trait of this placement is a dislike of complication. Those who are born with the Sun in this position prefer a straightforward life; they loathe deceit, and they need to see that the motives of those around them are clear and transparent.

Meaning: The Three of Clubs may be a card of potential success, but it has a definite downside. When this card is drawn, you can be sure that the better you do, the more your success will give rise to envy, backbiting, and overt hostility, often from people who ought to know better. It may be that an oversight or badly thought-out action will bring about this unpleasant episode, but even so it hardly seems just. Now it is up to the questioner. Is he going to take offense, react harshly, and declare the envious one an enemy for all eternity, thus creating a feud? Or is he going to rise above the slight, prove himself a better person, and continue enjoying his life and the success he has achieved? It is a very good question.

The Three of Diamonds

*"You that have drawn the number three
Great honor will your fortune be;
But if a female draw the same,
She must beware of fickle shame."*

Keyword: Documents.

Astrological Relationship: Mars in Capricorn. The masculine force of Mars is usually expressed as ambition and self-reliance. In Capricorn there is an indication of striving to achieve great things and a preoccupation with success and status. The negative side to this is a tendency to become cold, distant, and aloof. Wastefulness is rarely, if ever, tolerated.

Meaning: There are two major themes in the Diamonds suit. Money is the most obvious, but it is closely followed by communications. The Three emphasizes both themes, so you can be sure that when this card appears, important documentation will soon become an issue. The documents in question may relate to something legal or official, such as a will or a contract. A clue to the exact nature of the document may be found in the card to the immediate right of the Three of Diamonds. However, if no card at all appears in this position, then it is an indication of confusion, delays, and potential disputes.

The Three of Spades

"Thou that art happy in this trey
Shalt surely wed a lady gay;
Whilst maids who now the same shall take,
Join marriage with a poor town rake."

Keywords: Hasty words.

Astrological Relationship: Saturn in Libra. Saturn is considered the grimmest of the planets, but when in Libra its influence does tend to lighten up just a little. Saturn is considered to be "exalted" in the sign of the balance. The main emphasis is on absolute truth at all costs, even if facing up to things does involve a little pain. Saturn in Libra stands for holding to a point of principle, even at the cost of personal relationships.

Meaning: The Three of Spades depicts a frustrating situation that has gone on for a long time. Throughout this irritating period the questioner has held his tongue and not expressed his opinion for fear of making a bad situation worse. The trouble is that this can only go on for so long; eventually the questioner's temper will reach the boiling point, and words will spill out without restraint, usually in the most awkward of circumstances.

In a more general sense, the Three of Spades urges thought before action. It may indicate troubling news or could show that the questioner is unsure how to react to a particular incident. The patience indicated by Saturn is the key here. When the questioner is in doubt, he should do nothing! He should wait and see what happens next, because he can be sure that if he takes immediate action, the situation will become more complex and troubling.

The Three of Hearts

"The man who gets hold of this trey
Always bound, always obey;
A woman that shall draw this sort
Will sure drink brandy by the quart."

Keywords: Hasty promises.

Astrological Relationship: Mercury in Cancer. Mercury is considered an intellectual planet, but it is regarded as being weak when in an emotional, watery sign such as Cancer. However, this placement does boost the powers of recall as well as stimulating the intuition. There is a danger of obsessive behavior when the planet of the mind (Mercury) becomes so closely attached to the emotions. Equally, there is a possibility that the fickleness of the mercurial nature will make the emotions shallow.

Meaning: When passions rise, words can come spilling from the lips in a gush of emotion. Whether these words are meant or not is another matter entirely. That is the message of the Three of Hearts. It may be that promises are made which in the cold light of day are instantly regretted. On the other hand, an argument between lovers may escalate into a full-blown quarrel during which certain things are said that cannot easily be retracted. Thus, the Three of Hearts can indicate disappointments in love.

As with the Three of Spades, thoughtless words and actions can have serious and far-reaching consequences.

6

The Fours

Four is symbolically considered to be either connected to the setting Sun or with the Earth itself. It is the earthy symbolism that is the most eloquent, because it implies hard work, practicality, and salt-of-the-earth virtues. The number implies that we are symbolically at the center, with the four directions—north, south, east, and west—radiating outward from us. In terms of time, four expresses the four seasons of spring, summer, fall, and winter. In ancient beliefs, we and everything around us are made up of the four elements of Fire, Earth, Air, and Water, or to put it in more modern terms, the four states of matter, plasma, solid, gaseous, and liquid. This is symbolically true of a deck of cards as well, with its Clubs, Diamonds, Spades, and Hearts.

The Four of Clubs

*"Now by this four we plainly see
Four children will be born to thee;
And she that draws the same shall wed
Two wealthy husbands, both well-bred."*

Traditional Name: Occasionally this card, like the Four of Spades, is referred to as the "Devil's Bedposts."

Keyword: Assistance.

Astrological Relationship: Venus in Aries. Venus, the planet of love, combines with fiery Aries to create an influence that is lively, creative, impulsive, and passionate. Amorous adventure comes easily to a person governed by this planetary influence. However, there is a strong tendency to rule the roost within a relationship when the usually gentle Venus gets a grip on the Arian battering-ram!

Meaning: Hardened card players tended to think that a hand that contained the Four of Clubs was an ill omen. This is surprising when one considers that the card has such a good interpretation in the traditions of card reading. When it appears in a spread, the message is that help is available to the questioner, whether assistance is actually needed or not. The implication is that the questioner is respected by his friends and colleagues. It also means that the questioner is probably unaware of the esteem in which he is held.

The only possible downside to the card is that the questioner may be so independent that he will refuse help when it is offered. Alternatively, he may be somewhat emotionally repressed and have difficulty in expressing his feelings.

The Four of Diamonds

"The man that draws the number four
Shall quite forsake his native shore;
But if the same a woman finds,
Both hand and heart in love she joins."

Keywords: Patient effort.

Astrological Relationship: Sun in Capricorn. Although there is an aura of toughness about the placement of the Sun in this sign, there is usually a deep emotional insecurity lurking beneath the capable exterior. This solar position indicates a tenacious, ambitious, opinionated, and somewhat unforgiving nature concealing a vulnerability that seeks solace in material possessions.

Meaning: The Four of Diamonds is not an exciting card; in fact it implies a period of slow, steady effort toward a specific goal. It is likely that this goal is financial in nature or may be connected with property. As a card of advice, the message is to tighten the belt, not spend so much on luxuries and entertainments, to be thrifty, to work hard, and pay attention to the use of cash. This strategy will pay off in a big way. So remember that when the Four of Diamonds appears in a reading, some sacrifices should be made, greater efforts should be employed, and a shrewder outlook put in place. The rewards for the questioner's efforts will be very great indeed.

The Four of Spades

"Now this same four betokens you
Shall lead a dissipated crew;
Maids that do draw the same shall meet
With certain joys always complete."

Keywords: Peace and quiet.

Astrological Relationship: Jupiter in Libra. Jupiter governs the concepts of spirituality and philosophy, among other things. When found in Libra these concepts are intimately connected with personal relationships. The path of self-discovery (which is usually thought of as a solitary one) is here expressed in social settings among friends and colleagues. Could this indicate the feeling of being lonely in a crowd?

Meaning: This is undoubtedly the most harmonious card in the Spades suit. This card signifies a respite from the trials and tribulations of life. It is likely that there has been a very stressful period in the questioner's life, and the appearance of the Four of Spades gives a breathing space, a chance to slow down, to reassess his position and to recover his depleted energies. This time is desperately necessary, if only to give his nerves a rest and to work out where he goes from here. However, there is a hint of warning here, because if the questioner (for whatever reason) does not intend to slow down at all, then a period during which he can reflect will be forced upon him. Thus the Four of Spades can denote stress-related ailments.

The Four of Hearts

"He that draws this four shall make
A faithful love for conscience sake;
But if it's drawn by womankind,
They will prove false, and that you'll find."

Keyword: Kindness.

Astrological Relationship: Moon in Cancer. The Moon is the planetary ruler of the sign of the Crab and it is very powerful here, being described as "dignified." Intuitive, very sensitive, and quite moody, this influence is family oriented, clannish, and home loving. The lunar influence here adds a maternal, protective, and caring element.

Meaning: The Four of Hearts is a charitable card. It signifies that the questioner will help others with no thought of reward for himself. It shows a period when his self-interest should take second place to the needs of others. Although this seems to imply self-sacrifice for the greater good, it will not actually be like that, because the questioner will gain personal satisfaction and a new self-knowledge from the help that he gives. The subsidiary meanings of the card reflect this aspect of the Four of Hearts, because it also means working in a happy and contented environment. This combines with the feeling that the questioner is doing something worthwhile rather than simply getting on with it for the sake of a paycheck.

7

The Fives

Five is the number associated with that most communicative, restless, nervy, and intellectual of planets, Mercury. Five is considered to be the most changeable of numbers because it is the halfway point of the single digits. Its influence is lively, and it encourages the search for new experiences and novelty in all forms. It may be regarded as an impish force, mischievous and eternally curious. Five is the number of the mystical pentagram, the five-pointed star, four points of which symbolize the four elements of Fire, Earth, Air, and Water, and the fifth point representing the soul or the mind of man.

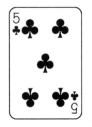

The Five of Clubs

"Now by this five 'tis clear to see
Thy wife will but a slattern be.
This same five drawn by virgins, they
Shall all wed husbands kind and gay."

Keyword: Friction.

Astrological Relationship: Saturn in Leo. There is a conflict here between the sobering influence of Saturn and the exuberance of the sign of the Lion. This gives a desire for the best quality in everything. The determination to achieve this in an imperfect world can cause problems, especially when one aims too high for ideals that are implausible. The real downside of this placement is a tendency toward pomposity.

Meaning: Traditional interpretations of this card state that the Five of Clubs means a heated argument between friends. The underlying causes of this conflict may never actually get as far as heated words, but nonetheless, they are troubling. The main reason for any disagreement is likely to be envy—although it is not uncommon for both persons to flatly deny this emotion. It is likely that one of the friends has progressed faster, earns more money, and lives in a better house. Perhaps he drives a better car or possesses something else that could provoke the "green-eyed monster." The sad fact of the matter is that both parties could actually be secretly envious of each other, each seeing in the other's lifestyle what is lacking in their own.

As a card of advice, the Five of Clubs urges the questioner not to be pompous or boastful.

The Five of Diamonds

"He that draweth the number five,
Where he was born he best will thrive;
But if it's drawn by womankind,
Good luck abroad they sure will find."

Keywords: Business conflicts.

Astrological Relationship: Mercury in Taurus. The fickle, changeable nature of Mercury is not comfortable in the slow, steady sign of Taurus. Impulsive moves and sudden decisions will cause far more problems than they solve. Equally, an attitude that is too inflexible will solve nothing. The balance between these two contradictory attitudes is difficult to achieve.

Meaning: The Five of Diamonds concerns money and business, but the outlook is not very good. There is likely to be a difference of opinion about exactly how one should move forward, and both points of view will be inflexible to the extreme. The astrological symbolism of the card gives a clue. One side of the argument is likely to be far more adventurous and impatient than the sober, cautious views of the other. A period of stalemate is reached and it may require intervention by an outsider to resolve the conflict.

In a more general sense, the Five of Diamonds could simply indicate a rapid series of changes in the questioner's financial fortunes. Cards surrounding this five should give more details.

The Five of Spades

"The five of spades gives you to know
That you must through some troubles go;
But, if a woman, it foretells
Her virtue others' far excels."

Keywords: Breaking free, tears.

Astrological Relationship: Venus in Aquarius. The love planet in the highly idealistic sign of Aquarius will certainly promote popularity, but it will also promote a desire to believe in fantasies. In relationship and business matters this can lead to terrible disappointments and feelings of resentment once the glitter fades. Frequent changes in fortune are associated with Venus in Aquarius.

Meaning: The Five of Spades is a traumatic card. The events that it foretells are difficult to cope with. They will cause self-questioning, doubts, regrets, and grief. It is also a card of separation from loved ones and from circumstances that were once comfortable and that are no longer so. It is likely that it is the questioner's own decisions have caused this separation, perhaps because he felt trapped, unloved, restricted, and generally beaten down by stress and worry. This card is associated with divorce, although a marital breakup is not necessarily the interpretation one should give in a reading. In many ways the card shows a flight to safety. The card to the immediate right—or at least near to the Five of Spades—should reveal whether the outcome of this flight will be good or bad.

The Five of Hearts

"Note that this five of hearts declares
Thou shalt well manage great affairs;
But if it's drawn by womankind,
They will prove false and that you'll find."

Keyword: Disappointment.

Astrological Relationship: Mars in Scorpio. Mars is traditionally held to be the ancient ruler of Scorpio, even though these days the honor tends to go to Pluto. Here the aggressive tendencies of the red planet are not overt; they are often expressed secretly and ruthlessly. Past offenses are not easily forgotten, and someone strongly influenced by this placement may spend a lot of time plotting revenge.

Meaning: The Five of Hearts is the most disruptive of this usually gentle suit. It has disturbing implications for relationships and it can mean that something that was once precious is drawing to a close. It is easy to see that this could be interpreted as the end of a love affair, but it could mean that it is time to let go of a long-held ambition that once meant a great deal on an emotional level. The good news is that the setback indicated by the Five of Hearts is a temporary one. As with any loss, there will be a period of mourning and self-doubt, but it will not be long before the questioner is back to his normal self, ready to face new challenges with renewed enthusiasm.

8

The Sixes

The number Six is connected to caring in all its forms. It is symbolically governed by the planet Venus, and it relates primarily to home and family issues. The number Six indicates a return of harmony and it can help to balance difficult, contentious situations. Diplomacy is another concept that is attached to this number, as indeed are sympathy, understanding, and thoughtfulness toward others. However, there is also a need for perfection, and there may be a tendency to take on too much responsibility when the Sixes are prominent in a reading.

The Six of Clubs

"By this six thou 'rt wed, we know,
To one that over thee will crow;
Maids that draw the same shall be
Blest with good husbands, kind and free."

Keywords: Happy meetings.

Astrological Relationship: Jupiter in Leo. This is an exuberant, optimistic, and creative placement for the giant planet. It gives genuine leadership ability but also a tendency to be bossy. Those influenced by Jupiter in the sign of the Lion think big, manage to accomplish extraordinary things, and also overcome seemingly impossible odds simply because failure is not an option.

Meaning: The Six of Clubs is a happy card indicating an active social life and lots of fun. More importantly, it also shows meetings with new people who will be a positive influence in future life. In some cases, the appearance of this card indicates a coming together of two people in a romantic sense (if the Six of Clubs is surrounded by Hearts). In another sense, the card could indicate the formation of a business partnership or a friend giving the questioner the opportunity of taking a good job.

If the questioner is divorced, this card could point to the establishment of a new and far better relationship. If he is unemployed, then the right job will soon turn up. If there has been quarreling in the family, reconciliation is now a strong possibility. In all ways, the Six of Clubs is a welcome sight in any reading because it points toward improvements in friendships, romance, and career prospects.

Lenormand Number and Symbol: 36; Cross.

The Six of Diamonds

"He that can catch the number six
Will have cunning and crafty tricks;
But if a woman draw the same,
Twill show that she is free from blame."

Keyword: Patience.

Astrological Relationship: Moon in Taurus. The Moon is ever changing, yet it achieves its maximum stability in the sign of the Bull. This is an indicator of prosperity as well as financial and emotional support from family and friends. The main influence of this lunar placement is the establishment of firm values on which to base decisions that will promote financial security.

Meaning: Although the financial picture is not likely to be a rosy one, the appearance of the Six of Diamonds suggests that there is a glimmer of light at the end of the tunnel. This is an optimistic card, especially when related to financial or property matters. It indicates a general improvement in circumstances, and that many of the questioner's anxieties will eventually fade, as the world adjusts itself to be more conducive to his happiness. It is at this point that his companions and his family will unexpectedly offer help and advice that might have been extremely useful if they had come up with it only a short while ago.

After this transformation has taken place, the questioner will find that his mind is clearer and that he has a better vision of where he wants to be. As a card of advice, the Six of Diamonds urges patience.

Lenormand Number and Symbol: 2; Clover.

The Six of Spades

"The six foretells whene'er you wed
You'll find your expectations fled;
But if a maid the number own
She'll wed a man of high renown."

Keyword: Anxiety.

Astrological Relationship: Mercury in Aquarius. Mercury is considered to be the planet of the mind, so it perfectly at home in the cool, idealistic sign of Aquarius. Here it gives the ability to rationalize worries and to examine options in a calm way, hopefully arriving at a reasonable solution. All one has to do then is put these marvelous ideas into practice!

Meaning: There is a proverb that goes "When poverty knocks on the door, love flies out the window" and that is the real message of this card. As usual, the Spades spell out bad news. In this case, the Six provides a warning for the questioner's personal and domestic life, for his finances and career. It looks as if disaster looms, yet this timely warning may prevent the questioner sinking beneath the vast weight of his problems.

It is inevitable that a financial worry will be knocking. Therefore, something has to be done—and quickly—though there is no cause to panic. The questioner should try to be cool and to look at the problem in a calm, logical frame of mind. If he cannot come up with a solution, then he should take advice, consult someone who can, and then act on it.

In another sense, the Six of Spades indicates conflict and lack of cooperation.

Lenormand Number and Symbol: 19; Tower.

The Six of Hearts

"The six of hearts surely foretells
Thou shalt be where great honor dwells;
If it falls on the other side
It then betokens scorn and pride."

Keyword: Panic.

Astrological Relationship: Sun in Scorpio. The Sun in the sign of the Scorpion indicates a loyal nature, but this loyalty is often restricted to members of the subject's own clan. A person with this influence makes an excellent friend and a bad enemy. This is an influence that promotes strong likes and dislikes. There are no half measures here! Scorpio is symbolically connected to the depths of the mind. Its modern ruler is Pluto, so it is named after the lord of the underworld. This suggests deep psychological drives stretching back into childhood experiences.

Meaning: The pressure is on emotional life when the Six of Hearts is prominent in a reading. Circumstances in the questioner's life will be difficult, and this is unlikely to be a surprise. The situation may be complicated by the fact that the questioner's family and friends—far from helping at this critical time—are preoccupied with their own concerns and they refuse to acknowledge the problems that the questioner is trying to solve. This could also mean that someone who is close to the questioner is draining his resources both in a financial and an emotional sense.

It is obvious that sensible decisions now have to be made, but hasty actions without due caution could make things much worse. As a card of advice, the Six of Hearts urges the questioner not to panic. He should remain calm and think everything through slowly and carefully. Only when the questioner has subdued his unruly emotions can he do anything practical.

Lenormand Number and Symbol: 16; Stars.

9

The Sevens

Lucky Seven is associated with the Full Moon. It represents a culmination of a phase, growing up, and an accumulation of experience and wisdom. This is regarded as a spiritual number of introspection and deep thought about the nature of the universe and one's own place in it. In essence, the approach it encourages is totally unique, unconventional, and even eccentric. The prominence of this number gives moments of clarity and insight that others cannot see, and a consequent decision-making process that others simply cannot follow.

The Seven of Clubs

"Thou hast now the seven drawn
Shall put thy Sunday clothes in pawn;
Maids that draw the same shall wear
Jewels rich without compare."

Keywords: Warning of danger ahead.

Astrological Relationship: Mars in Leo. The placement of the masculine Mars in the royal sign of Leo gives tremendous self-confidence. The concept of defeat is not one that is easily entertained by someone with this strong martial influence. Other features are organizational ability—marshalling one's forces, so to speak—and exceptional leadership qualities.

Meaning: This must be one of the most sexually discriminatory cards in the deck! It warns that if the questioner allows a member of the opposite sex any influence in business affairs, then these interests will be ruined. The only safety is in trusting those of one's own gender.

The Seven of Clubs tells of a period of minor delays and foulups that cannot be avoided but have to be borne with patience and resignation. (The Mars influence on the card implies fury rather than patience.) Nothing is likely to be too serious a problem, unless the Seven of Clubs is surrounded by grim cards, in which case there is a definite warning of danger ahead. Even so, it might be wise to seek some professional advice before proceeding with one's plans.

The card might even be taken as a form of criticism, especially if it is one of the first three cards drawn. It could show that the questioner is full of big ideas and that he is a great one for starting projects, but that he is not good at finishing them.

This Seven is likely to show that a time of forced learning is coming up in which the questioner has to take in a lot of information in a short time if he is to protect his interests.

Lenormand Number and Symbol: 23; Mouse.

The Seven of Diamonds

"Since that seven does appear,
Crosses thou hast cause to fear;
Women, whene'er the same they draw,
Shall not fear crosses more than straw."

Keywords: Warnings about money matters, envy, and gossip.

Astrological Relationship: Saturn in Taurus. The key concept connected with both slow-moving Saturn and steady Taurus is that of patience. It is true that Saturn may provide many setbacks and hitches, yet when it is in the materialistic sign of Taurus, its influence indicates that slow, painstaking effort is required to make the best of any situation.

Meaning: This is not a good card for financial dealings. The Seven of Diamonds must be taken as a warning not to take risks, especially with money. Therefore, speculating on the stock market, property deals, gambling, and even lending a few bucks to a friend are out.

Another unfortunate aspect of the card is that it reveals that the questioner is the victim of malicious gossip intended to ruin his reputation and spoil his prospects. The usual reason for a campaign of this sort is envy, so the card could be taken as a sort of backhanded compliment. The questioner has obviously done well so far; otherwise he would not be envied.

The problems revealed by the Seven of Diamonds are likely to be merely a passing phase. They will soon be over, especially if the questioner is willing to knuckle down to practicalities.

The cards on either side of the Seven of Diamonds will reveal where delays and setbacks are likely to occur.

Lenormand Number and Symbol: 12; Birds.

The Seven of Spades

"Now as the seven comes to hand,
It does entitle you to land;
But maids with this shall wed with those
That have no money, friends, or clothes."

Keywords: The eye of the storm.

Astrological Relationship: Moon in Aquarius. The unstable emotions governed by the Moon are strangely muted when in cool Aquarius. There is an air of detachment that leads to the suspicion of an unfeeling nature or lack of empathy.

Meaning: A turbulent, overly emotional atmosphere surrounds the questioner when the Seven of Spades is prominent in a reading. The questioner must keep his cool against all odds and provocations. The questioner may feel powerless simply because he cannot get his point of view across. The best action for the questioner to take is to avoid trying to convince others of the rightness of his actions. Everything he says will be twisted and willfully misunderstood so that he becomes the villain of the piece in other people's eyes, even if he is completely innocent of wrongdoing.

In a wider sense, the Seven of Spades warns against making far-reaching business decisions because it flatly states that there are hidden factors. In addition, the questioner's judgment is likely to be faulty at this time because his heated imagination takes the place of solid facts.

Having said the foregoing, the card does promise great success in the future, after a period of persistence.

Lenormand Number and Symbol: 27; Letter.

The Seven of Hearts

"Now this old seven, I'll maintain,
Shows that thou hast not loved in vain;
Thou shalt obtain the golden prize,
But, with the maids, 'tis otherwise."

Keywords: Lover's tiff.

Astrological Relationship: Venus in Scorpio. The Scorpion takes on a gentler mood in the presence of Venus, as passion and sensuality are mingled together. However, when passion is spent, the Scorpion may reassert its vengeful nature and strike with its deadly sting. The old saying goes: "Hell hath no fury like a woman scorned." In this case, it is the Venus in Scorpio aspect of the Seven of Hearts that gives cause for concern!

Meaning: A lover's quarrel is the most commonly accepted meaning of this card. However, unless the Seven of Hearts is surrounded by particularly grim cards, this disagreement is likely to be fairly minor and will be over just as quickly as it started. The deep emotions that are signified by the Hearts hold true; thus love will not only survive, but it will not have been in any real danger. Following this reasoning, the card may show a temporary parting, possibly (but not necessarily) caused by a tiff. If love is not the issue, then the questioner will be let down in some personal matter by an unreliable friend or colleague.

The Seven of Hearts does not bode well for business dealings and it recommends the avoidance of get-rich-quick schemes and shady characters.

If the Seven of Hearts is among the first three cards in a spread, it is likely that the questioner is too trusting and gullible. He is advised to be more assertive and self-confident in appearance.

Lenormand Number and Symbol: 5; Tree.

10

The Eights

The number Eight is connected with materialism in its widest sense. Eight is governed by the ringed orb of Saturn—the harsh, grim taskmaster of the planetary crew. However, Saturn is not always bad news. There may be an inclination to be stubborn, rigid in outlook, and singleminded in purpose, but there is no doubt that these qualities, combined with patience and perseverance, get things done! A predominance of Eights will lead to success in due time. Eight may not be the most exciting of numbers, but it promotes solid, steady progress toward status and high achievement.

The Eight of Clubs

"By this club eight, tho' Whig or Tory,
Thy life will prove a tragic story;
Ye maids that draw the same, are born
To hold both fools and fops in scorn."

Keywords: Peace and harmony.

Astrological Relationship: Mercury in Sagittarius. The fleet-footed Mercury is at home in the sign of the Archer, who is a lover of far-distant travel, excitement, and exploration. This placement implies many interests, versatility, and a tendency toward restlessness and impulsive decision making. However, there is also the ability to grasp complex matters quickly, in addition to perceiving the hidden meanings within a message.

Meaning: This card is good news for those who are ground down by work and duty. The Eight of Clubs tells the questioner to take a break, and it suggests that there is more to life than the rat race. This is especially true if this is one of the first three cards in a spread.

The card is an indicator of the return of peace of mind. Worry will fade. It will not disappear altogether, but the questioner will begin to realize that there is more to life than his petty personal concerns. If too much emphasis has been placed on material values there will now be a change of viewpoint.

The card suggests a journey or a voyage of discovery. The main thing to discover here is the questioner's own true self and his path to inner tranquility.

Lenormand Number and Symbol: 21; Mountain.

The Eight of Diamonds

"Hast thou drawn the number eight?
Thou sure will be a rascal great;
Females that chance the same to take,
They never will the truth forsake."

Keywords: Material success.

Astrological Relationship: Sun in Virgo. Virgo is associated with attention to detail, foresight, and practicality. This placement indicates a good, dutiful employee, a diligent servant, and a shrewd analyst of situations and people. However there is an equal tendency to be fussy and critical of oneself and others.

Meaning: The Eight of Diamonds is an excellent indicator of financial good fortune, especially if it occurs early in a reading. Practicality is the key to success when this Eight appears. If the questioner can approach all problems with a firm grip on the realities of life, then he will achieve all that he desires. This includes health issues, for the card advises plenty of rest and recuperation after strenuous efforts.

Sometimes the Eight of Diamonds indicates an extraordinary triumph. The surrounding cards will show whether this is the case or not. If it is the case, the innate practicality indicated by the card must come into play, urging the questioner not to allow success go to his head.

Lenormand Number and Symbol: 33; Key.

The Eight of Spades

"This eight of spades foretells you shall
Wed a young maid fair, straight, and tall;
If to a maid the same shall come,
She weds the brother of Tom Thumb."

Keywords: Impaired judgment.

Astrological Relationship: Jupiter in Gemini. The giant planet is in "detriment" in the sign of the twins, so the footloose and fancy-free nature of Jupiter is likely to be trapped and restricted by petty matters when it is found here. Intellectual pursuits and travel are indicated, but they somehow seem to be lacking in scope. The general feeling of this placement is quite frustrating.

Meaning: There are two sides to the Eight of Spades. On the one hand it signifies joy, which is a rare interpretation in the Spades suit. However, as might be expected, this joy usually means that something horrible has just ended, so it is really a sense of relief that the nastiness is over.

Another interpretation indicates that the questioner is now out of trouble, but that he maintains a residual feeling that it will all start up again very soon, even if there is no real likelihood of the previous problem recurring.

The only problem remaining is a tendency to let off steam, to allow standards to slip or disappear altogether. The questioner may overindulge himself, and thus land back in a mess similar to that which he has so recently escaped. This sort of reactive behavior is likely to cause misunderstandings and arguments with old friends.

Lenormand Number and Symbol: 20; Garden.

The Eight of Hearts

"Having drawn the number eight,
Shows thou'rt servile, born to wait;
But if a woman draw the same,
She'll mount upon the wings of fame."

Keywords: A love gift.

Astrological Relationship: Saturn in Pisces. The duty-oriented Saturn is not in tune with dreamy, idealistic Pisces. The world of harsh practical reality and that of daydreams are so far apart that a conflict between them is inevitable. Saturn here can cause self-undoing through overemotionalism and failure to grasp realities.

Meaning: It is said that it is better to give than to receive, but in the case of the Eight of Hearts, a gift that is given to the questioner will be very welcome indeed. This need not be in the form of anything material (although it often is) but rather a sort of peace offering or a gesture of affection.

This is a card of true friendship, of healing rifts, of forgetting of old wounds, and the establishment of something wonderfully, emotionally fulfilling. The Eight of Hearts also implies that affection is not a one-way street—so the questioner must give something in return. In most cases this will be done gladly, and this offer of love, peace, and friendship will be wholeheartedly accepted and reciprocated.

Lenormand Number and Symbol: 32; Moon.

11

The Nines

Nine is the number of aggressive Mars. Thus, like its celestial counterpart, it has a restless nature. Nine gives us the urge to explore, to seek out new experiences, and to experiment with life. Nine is at its most effective when there is a purpose in mind, because otherwise many of the powerful energies that are inherent in the number are aimlessly frittered away. Another aspect of the number's influence is that of humanitarianism—a kindness and a sense of duty to humanity. This does not mean that it is directed toward any one person, but to the world in general. Much of the satisfaction gained by using the number Nine energy comes from giving— although this may not be immediately evident when there is a preponderance of Nines in a reading.

Notes: The Curse of Scotland

The Nine of Diamonds is known as the "Curse of Scotland" even though its divinatory meaning is positive, implying that the questioner's desires will come to pass. Various explanations have been given for this dire title, which was first recorded in the 18th century. It has been suggested that the back of the card was used to convey disastrous battle orders. King James IV is said to have sketched the fatal disposition of his forces on this card before the terrible Battle of Flodden in 1513. Likewise the English commander (the "Butcher of Cumberland") at the equally appalling Battle of Culloden (1746) is said to have done the same, as did the bloodthirsty Earl of Stair before the Glencoe Massacre in 1692. The fact that this particular Earl used a heraldic shield bearing nine red lozenges may be the origin of this story.

Another tragic figure of Scottish history is also associated with the Nine of Diamonds—Mary, Queen of Scots, who introduced sophisticated card games from the decadent court of France to her puritanical northern kingdom. She is said to have drawn the fateful card on the night before her execution. It is odd that Mary of Scotland was a lady who showed marked Venusian characteristics, while she died in the realm of her cousin, the virginal Elizabeth I. This eerily reflects the astrological associations of this card: Venus in Virgo.

The Nine of Diamonds was also nicknamed "The Pope" in a once popular game called "Pope Joan." This Catholic title was hardly likely to warm the hearts of the strictly protestant Scots at that time of religious ferment.

A more prosaic explanation may be that the word "curse" is actually a corruption of "cross," since the diamonds on the card were often arranged in a "saltire," the pattern of St. Andrew's cross, which is on the flag of Scotland.

The Nine of Clubs

"By this brave nine, upon my life,
You soon shall wed a wealthy wife;
She that shall draw the same shall have
One that is both fool and knave."

Keywords: The card of contentment.

Astrological Relationship: Moon in Sagittarius. This placement is associated with the practical application of learned wisdom. The straightforward influence of the Archer will always be preferred to underhanded schemes. There are deep emotional resources available, and a person who is influenced by this lunar placement will be very resilient in the face of opposition.

Meaning: A feeling of personal achievement and self-satisfaction is revealed by the Nine of Clubs. Whatever the questioner's goals and desires happen to be, when this card appears in a reading, one can be sure that he has taken a step closer to fulfillment. This is a card of progress, moving toward a desired goal. It is possible that one more hurdle has to be dealt with before final success is achieved, but this should not be too difficult, and the well-deserved end is in sight. It is also likely that the questioner is aware of this fact, and is already looking around for new challenges that will follow his triumph.

On a social level, enjoyment within a closely-knit group of like-minded people is indicated.

Lenormand Number and Symbol: 14; Fox.

The Nine of Diamonds

"Hast thou turn'd up the merry nine?
Then guineas will thy pocket line;
She that doth draw it to her hand
Will die for love or leave the land."

Traditional Name: The Curse of Scotland.

Keywords: Revelation and treachery.

Astrological Relationship: Venus in Virgo. The planet of love in the sign of the virgin? It doesn't seem right—yet here it is. This hints at some serious disappointments in the person's love life! On the more positive side, there are considerable business abilities and communication skills at work here. Work in areas such as health or beauty is favored by this placement.

Meaning: On the surface, the meaning of the Nine of Diamonds is a positive one, because it states that whatever the questioner wishes for will come true. However, this is not as good as it seems, because the card also has connotations of danger, deceit, and unwanted complications. Madamoiselle Lenormand believed that this card was indicative of a self-seeking, dishonest rogue or a traitor. Therefore the questioner would be wise to be on his guard, because all is not as it seems.

In a way, the Nine of Diamonds reveals a situation in which the questioner can deceive himself into believing what he wants to believe rather than seeing the facts. It also hints that whatever it is that is desired should be worthwhile, honest, and beyond reproach. If it is not, the questioner will wish that he had never wanted it in the first place due to the trouble that it will inevitably bring.

Lenormand Number and Symbol: 8; Coffin.

The Nine of Spades

"Now by this nine thou art foretold,
Thou shalt wed one deaf, lame, and old.
Females, when they draw this odd chance,
Shall of themselves to wealth advance."

Keywords: The card of disappointment.

Astrological Relationship: Mars in Gemini. There is an instinctive dread of being trapped or restricted when Mars is found in Gemini. A refusal to take into account other people's expectations is a common trait, as well as a tendency to follow one's own whims without thinking things through properly. The inner turmoil of the mind can turn into aggression and confrontation.

Meaning: The Nine of Spades has the reputation of being one of the worst cards in the deck. Its appearance signals the end of a way of life, a collapse of previously held beliefs, and the consequent feelings of total dejection. However, this grim outlook is only part of the story, because this card—unpleasant as it is—provides a clean slate, an opportunity for a fresh start.

This card indicates a forced change that will be unwelcome when it comes. The major changes that the card reveals are inevitable, and it is probable that they have been coming for some time. These upheavals will force the questioner to abandon selfish ways and to become more thoughtful and considerate of the feelings of others.

Lenormand Number and Symbol: 35; Anchor.

The Nine of Hearts

"By this long nine be well assured
That lovesick pains must be endured;
But the maid that draws this nine
Soon in wedlock hands shall join."

Traditional Name: The wish card.

Keywords: Good luck.

Astrological Relationship: Jupiter in Pisces. Jupiter was previously considered to be the ruler of this sign. This placement promotes imagination, artistic gifts, humanity, generosity, and a romantic nature. It is associated with optimism, fun, and laughter. Jupiter is considered to be the "luck-bringer" so it is a very apt association for the Nine of Hearts, the "wish card."

Meaning: This is traditionally considered to be a very lucky omen. The Nine of Hearts is one of the best cards in the deck; this is why it is called the "wish card." When found in a future position within a reading, the questioner can be assured that happiness lies in store, that everything is progressing as it should, and that he is on the right path to great satisfaction in all sectors of his life. He can also take pride in the fact that this new joy is well deserved; that he has helped other people and he is now reaping his karmic reward.

The Nine of Hearts also has a meaning of "yes" in some specific questions, as you will see in the chapter on general spreads.

Lenormand Number and Symbol: 1; Cavalier.

12

The Tens

As we reach the number Ten, we enter a new level. According to the rules of Pythagorean numerology, which does not recognize the existence of zero, this means that when we reach the number Ten, we actually return once more to number one. The rising Sun is the symbolic image of One, and now, it rises once again after a complete cycle of one day has been completed. So, another cycle begins.

With the Tens we reach the phase in which results are made manifest. Each card of each suit can be thought of as a stage in a process and a succession of events, of which the Ten shows both an end and a new beginning.

In other symbolism, Ten has a symbolic resonance of its own. There are the Ten Commandments that were carved on stone tablets, which Moses brought to the wandering people of Israel. In the Qabalah, a complex system of Hebrew mysticism, there are ten planes of existence, which are thought of as pure numbers that hang like fruit from the Tree of Life.

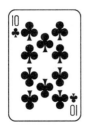

The Ten of Clubs

"Now for this number, half a score,
Shows that thou wilt be wretched poor;
Maids that do draw this number still
Shall have great joy and wealth at will."

Keywords: New beginnings.

Astrological Relationship: Saturn in Sagittarius. The gloomy nature of Saturn contrasts with the optimism of Sagittarius, and so the presence of the ringed planet could dampen the innate enthusiasm of the sign. However, the two influences can work well together, combining strength of purpose and single-mindedness with breadth of vision and a sense that all efforts are for some greater purpose. In the case of this card, the desire for exploration found in Sagittarius is employed to some practical goal—as implied by Saturn.

Meaning: The Ten of Clubs is a good omen for new beginnings. A new day has dawned, and with it comes the potential of new directions and challenges to be embraced. Because Clubs are often associated with work and effort, nothing will land easily in the questioner's lap, but all the factors are present to make a success of whatever he wants to do.

This is a card of enthusiasm. It may hint at a return to the excitement and sense of adventure associated with the Ace of this suit. However, this reawakening keenness should not go to the questioner's head; otherwise he will concentrate solely on his work. This would mean losing the friendships he develops within his working environment and neglecting his family and other well-established companions.

Lenormand Number and Symbol: 15; Bear.

The Ten of Diamonds

"O brave! The ten, 'tis very well!
There's none in love shall thee excel.
Only the maid who draws the ten
May wed, but nobody knows when."

Keyword: Materialism.

Astrological Relationship: Mercury in Virgo. Mercury, ruler of Virgo, is at its most analytical and precise when found in the sign. Problem solving is a great strength, as indeed is a swift, incisive, decision-making mental process. Physical well-being and health issues are also emphasized by this placement.

Meaning: The Ten of Diamonds signifies wealth and status but also boredom. Much has been achieved, but is this all there is to life? That is what the questioner may be asking himself when the Ten of Diamonds appears. The world may seem a very dull place, with routine and mind-numbing drudgery spoiling a comfortable existence.

Tens represent the end of a cycle and the beginning of a new one, so it is likely that new avenues are being sought when this card is prominent in a spread. If it is among the first three cards, then it is likely that the questioner is feeling pretty jaded and cynical. He is probably looking for something more than material comfort in order to put some meaning back into his life.

Lenormand Number and Symbol: 26; Book.

The Ten of Spades

"Tis seen by this long ten of spades
That thou shalt follow many trades,
And thrive by none. But women, they,
By this chance shall not work but play."

Keyword: Disillusionment.

Astrological Relationship: Sun in Gemini. On the surface it seems there is little connection between the Sun's position in Gemini and this gloomy card, but it should be remembered that Gemini is a dual sign, possessing two distinct natures. The dark side of Gemini features falsehood and isolation—these traits being in total contrast with the witty communication of the lighter half. Looking at it another way, this astral association could point to a turning point or a symbolic change over from dark to light. In short, as the old saying goes, "it is always darkest before the dawn."

Meaning: The Ten of Spades (along with the Nine of Spades) has a dreadful reputation in card reading tradition. Remember that Tens show the culmination of their respective suits, while Spades are always challenging, to say the least. The Ten of Spades represents an impassable barrier to progress. It suggests that the questioner has made great efforts in the past, but that he has now has come to a full stop and he can go no further in this direction. This realization may come as a shock, leading to a feeling of disillusionment and pointlessness.

It is time for a change, but it is likely that the questioner will resist this necessary alteration because he has worked so hard to get to this point. Now he must step back, reassess his situation, and decide which way he should go from here.

Lenormand Number and Symbol: 3; Ship.

The Ten of Hearts

"This ten it is a lucky cast,
For it doth show the worst is past;
But if the maids the same shall have,
Love will their tender hearts enslave."

Keywords: Good news.

Astrological Relationship: Mars in Pisces. The sequence of pip cards ends as it began with an association with the planet, Mars. This time the red planet is found in Pisces, which is the last sign of the zodiac. This is where the relentless drive of Mars turns inward or totally disappears. The need for strife has passed for the moment at least. The mood of this placement is gentle, intuitive and artistic. It may also indicate a self-sacrifice that is made for the greater good.

Meaning: The Ten of Hearts is the card of good news. This is likely to be something totally unexpected; though it seems that the questioner has already set events in motion that are culminating in this excellent development. The cards on either side of this one will reveal the nature of the glad tidings. The only possible downside to the card is that the tidings are likely to be so good that the questioner is in danger of becoming complacent once the pleasant surprise has worn off. There is an implied warning that this marvelous information sets off a new cycle, so the questioner should not be too self-satisfied or rest on his laurels for too long.

Lenormand Number and Symbol: 18; Dog.

13

The Jacks

The four Jacks, or Knaves, represent the mutable signs of the zodiac, Sagittarius, Virgo, Gemini, and Pisces. They can symbolize people of either sex, usually those who are youthful in mind or body.

In number symbolism, Jacks are allocated to Eleven. This is known as a "power number," but it tends to reveal potentials rather than results. When applied to people, the number Eleven can indicate an inferiority complex and self-absorption, which may be covered up by an arrogant, defiant, cocky attitude. Sensitivity to the needs of others should be developed. However, Eleven also bestows great originality of thinking, even if it does come at the price of discarding conventional values.

Each of the court cards (the Jacks, Queens, Kings) is associated with a sign of the zodiac and the time of year that the sign encompasses. These date-sensitive cards may help you to work out approximately when something will occur, or when a problem will be resolved.

The Jack of Clubs

"See how the surly knave appears!
Pray take care of both your ears!
Women, whene'er the same they see,
Will be what oft they used to be."

Traditional Name: The Jack of Clubs is given the identity of Sir Lancelot du Lac, the greatest knight in the entire world. Lancelot was the champion of King Arthur, but he betrayed his King's trust by his infidelity with Queen Guinevere.

Appearance: The Jack of Clubs is thought of as having dark hair and eyes, although not as dark as those of the Jack of Spades. This Jack is romantic and idealistic.

Astrological Relationship: The Jack is associated with the fiery mutable sign of Sagittarius the Archer (November 22 to December 21).

Meaning: The Jack of Clubs is a faithful friend; an honest and respectable person. He may represent a young man in love. If found next to a Heart or Diamond, his chances of romantic success are very good—unless that card happens to be the Jack of Hearts, in which case a dangerous rivalry is likely. An adjacent Club or Spade would denote a stalwart ally.

The Jack of Clubs has the questioner's best interests at heart and he is a thoughtful and helpful person. If the card is one of the first three drawn, it refers either to the questioner or to someone close by. If the questioner does not recognize the description, there is a dark man around who thinks well of him.

Lenormand Number and Symbol: 11; Birch.

The Jack of Diamonds

"Is now the Knave of Diamonds come?
Be sure beware the martial drum:
Yet if a woman draw the knave,
She shall better fortune have."

Traditional Name: This card is identified with Hector, the honorable Trojan hero who was slain by Achilles and then dragged behind his chariot around the walls of Troy. It was this shameful act that culminated in Achilles' own death at the hands of Hector's brother, Paris.

Appearance: This card represents a young person of either sex, usually with rich brown hair and dark eyes, although possibly also red or blond hair. It can also indicate a soldier or a person in uniform.

Astrological Relationship: The Jack of Diamonds is associated with the mutable sign of Virgo the Virgin (August 23 to September 22).

Meaning: The Jack of Diamonds can bring good news about money, travel for business, or a promotion. A youngster may do something that will make others proud (if the card is in an unfavorable position, then the opposite applies). This card brings bad news when drawn for a man, but good news for a woman.

The Jack of Diamonds symbolizes confusion, and while he gives the impression that all is well, he is beset by anxieties and uncertainty. Time is an important factor here, so it may take patience to resolve difficulties. If this card is one of the first three drawn, it represents the questioner or someone close by.

Lenormand Number and Symbol: 22; Scythe.

The Jack of Spades

"This is a knave, pray have a care
That you fall not into despair:
Women, who the same shall choose,
Shall prove great fools, but that's no news."

Traditional Name: Early French cardmakers assigned this Jack to Hogier the Dane, a mighty Scandinavian warrior who was once the enemy of the great emperor Charlemagne. The two eventually became staunch allies, and Hogier became the emperor's most formidable champion.

Appearance: This Jack is often very dark, both in hair and complexion. However, he could be extremely fair or very striking in some other way.

Astrological Relationship: The Jack is associated with the mutable, dual-natured sign of Gemini the Twins (May 21 to June 21).

Meaning: This Jack has a dubious reputation, connected to the idea of disgrace or bad behavior. It may indicate a troubled mind, betrayal in love or the loss of liberty. This is one of the "One-Eyed Jacks," so the Jack of Spades is a knave who chooses to show only one side of his complex character. He has a roguish charm, a ready wit, intelligence, and an eye on the main chance. He is determined and resourceful, even when all seems lost, because he will always bounce back, more cheeky and audacious than ever. He is a wonderful ally, but a dangerous enemy. If this is one of the first three cards drawn, it represents the questioner or someone close by.

Lenormand Number and Symbol: 13; Child.

The Jack of Hearts

"He that draws the Knave of Hearts
Betokens he hath knavish parts:
But if a woman draw the knave,
Of no man shall she be the slave."

Traditional Name: The Jack of Hearts is usually identified with *La Hire* (the hireling or mercenary). This is a historical figure called Etienne de Vignolles (1380–1442 A.D.). De Vignolles was a companion in arms of Joan of Arc. According to legend, the foul-mouthed Etienne gave up swearing under Joan's saintly influence! The card is also associated with the Roman god of love, Cupid, and his Christian equivalent, Saint Valentine.

Appearance: Good looking with a winning smile, the Jack of Hearts can turn heads and cause weakness in the knees. He is said to be fair with sparkling blue eyes, but he could be equally attractive in some other way.

Astrological Relationship: The Jack of Hearts is symbolized by the sign of Pisces the Fish, dwellers in the deep who swim in opposite directions (February 19 to March 20).

Meaning: In the children's rhyme, *the Jack of Hearts stole the tarts, he stole them right away…* In card readings, this Jack is a thief of hearts. He could be a fickle lover and a seducer. He is undoubtedly a charmer with a knack of getting away with it, and not only being forgiven, but also loved and admired. This is the second of the "One-Eyed Jacks" and he may wear a uniform for his work. He is involved in all matters of love and romance, but he can also denote a break from routine and a much needed holiday.

Lenormand Number and Symbol: 24; Heart.

14

The Queens

The emotional strength and reliability of the four Queens naturally allies them to the four fixed signs of the zodiac. The Queen of Clubs is fiery by nature, so she is associated with the zodiac sign of Leo the Lion. The materialistic, earthy Queen of Diamonds is represented by the stable sign of Taurus the Bull. The cool Queen of Spades is connected to the aloof sign of Aquarius the Water Bearer, and finally the deep and enigmatic Queen of Hearts attaches to the equally mysterious and alluring sign of Scorpio the Scorpion.

In numerology, the Queens are allocated the number Twelve. The most obvious symbolic association of Twelve is that it is the number of the signs of the zodiac. This represents a totality, a summing up, and a celestial circular framework within which all human action takes place. To take the zodiac imagery a little further, we should look at the twelfth house of the horoscope. This is an area that relates to caring, sympathy, impressionability, psychic awareness, and a readiness to sacrifice oneself for the sake of others.

Each of the court cards (i.e. the Jacks, Queens, Kings) is associated with a sign of the zodiac and the time of year that the sign encompasses. These date-sensitive cards may help you to work out approximately when something will occur, or when a problem will be resolved.

The Queen of Clubs

"If the Queen of Clubs thou hast,
Thou shalt be with great honor graced.
And women, if the same they find,
Will have things after their own mind."

Traditional Name: There is a mystery surrounding the name given to the Queen of Clubs by early card designers, as she was assigned the name "Argine," which is an anagram of "Regina." Any particular identity has been lost.

Appearance: This Queen has an olive or dark complexion and she is considered to be a lively character.

Astrological Relationship: The Queen of Clubs is fiery and creative, so she is symbolized by the sign of Leo, which runs from July 24 to August 23.

Meaning: The Queen of Clubs is sociable, outgoing, and friendly. She has great charm, grace, and elegance. She is a stylish dresser and she creates an attractive home. Beneath the façade is a shrewd, responsible businesswoman. This Queen can adjust to situations or work them to suit her own needs, but she is not coldly manipulative. She enjoys being the center of attention, but she can be moody, downhearted, and lonely at times.

When this card is among the first three dealt for a male, it represents an influential woman in his life. For a woman, it might represent her personality or the family or business challenges that she faces at the time of the reading.

Lenormand Number and Symbol: 7; Serpent.

The Queen of Diamonds
"Now is the Queen of Diamonds fair,
She shows thou shalt some office share;
Oh, woman! If it fall to you,
Friends you will have not a few."

Traditional Name: The Queen of Diamonds is usually called Rachel, the Biblical character who was the favorite wife of Jacob (Genesis 29: 1–30 and 35: 16–20). To win Rachel, Jacob worked for her father, Laban, for seven years, only to be tricked into marrying Rachel's sister, Leah. Jacob then had to work another seven years to gain his love, Rachel, who later gave birth to Joseph and Benjamin.

Appearance: The Queen of Diamonds represents a mature woman or someone who appears older or younger than her years. She is usually fair or gray haired with a pale complexion.

Astrological Relationship: This Queen is obstinate, practical, and earthy, just like her zodiac sign of Taurus the Bull (April 21 to May 21).

Meaning: The Queen of Diamonds has a dubious reputation, as she is said to be a rumormonger, and a frustrated and spiteful woman, but it may be that in olden days her passion for life and her capability had no outlet and were not appreciated. Now we appreciate her agile and decisive mind, her business acumen, and her sense of responsibility. She does not shrink from aggression or from creating public scenes.

This card may represent a good friend or it may indicate a need for more assertion.

Lenormand Number and Symbol: 22; Paths.

The Queen of Spades

*"Here is the Queen of Spades likewise
Thou soon shalt unto riches rise:
A woman by the same shall have
What her own heart doth surely crave."*

Traditional Name: This martial lady has been called Black Maria and Old Maid after card games of those names. She is identified with female warriors such as Joan of Arc and Boudicca. She has also been linked with Lucrezia Borgia who was wrongly accused of poisoning others. This Queen has also been named Bathsheba after the adulterous lover of King David, but most early French decks call the card "Pallas" after Pallas Athena, the Greek goddess of wisdom, who was usually depicted in armor, carrying a spear and shield, as shown on most versions of the card.

Appearance: This Queen is thought of as possessing dark hair and eyes. However, this symbolic darkness may be a reflection of the darkness within—a sadness that is never far from the surface. The card often represents a widow or someone in mourning.

Astrological Relationship: The cool, somewhat aloof character of the Queen of Spaces has been identified with the emotionally detached sign of Aquarius (January 20 to February 19).

Meaning: The basic interpretation of the card homes in on disappointment and loneliness. Although a widow figure, this Queen displays a remarkable stoicism and dignity in the face of adversity. She survives everything that the world throws at her, and she never forgives those who stand in her way. This woman is intriguing and mysterious, reserved, cautious, and deep. She may be recovering from some emotional trauma, but she is an excellent friend and a wise advisor to those whom she allows to get close to her.

If the questioner is a woman and this is one of the first three cards dealt, it refers to her, but if the questioner is male, it may represent his mother.

Lenormand Number and Symbol: 9; Flowers.

The Queen of Hearts

"Now by this card it is well known
Thou shalt enjoy still all thine own;
But women, if they draw the same,
Shall sure enjoy a happy name."

Traditional Name: Some early French decks dub this Queen Cleopatra, others call her Delilah or Helen of Troy, but she is most commonly associated with Judith. Judith was a devout widow in the town of Bethulia who abandoned her widow's weeds for fine clothes and jewelry in order to seduce the Assyrian general, Holofernes, who was intent on slaughtering the inhabitants of the town. When Holofernes became drunk, Judith cut off his head, after which the townspeople were able to defeat the Assyrian forces.

The Queen of Hearts can also be seen as Aphrodite or Venus, the goddess of love. The late Diana, Princess of Wales, wanted to be known as the Queen of Hearts, as did her distant ancestor Mary, Queen of Scots.

Appearance: The Queen of Hearts is beautiful with an artful charm. Traditionally fair with stunning blue eyes, she is usually delicate and superbly presented.

Astrological Relationship: The enigmatic Queen of Hearts is associated with passionate Scorpio (October 24 to November 22).

Meaning: The Queen of Hearts rules affairs of the heart and emotional vulnerability, but there may also be a need for the questioner to concentrate on creativity. The card indicates good fortune in love, affectionate friends and happy family life.

This Queen wants to love and be loved, and she works from the heart. She is intuitive, understanding, and sympathetic; she loves social life, fun, and laughter, and is adept at making small talk. She hates coarseness, ugliness, and bad taste. She is artistic, with excellent fashion sense and an eye for color and form.

Lenormand Number and Symbol: 17; Stork.

15

The Kings

The four King cards are symbolically associated with the four cardinal signs of the zodiac. The energetic King of Clubs is linked with the vitality of Aries the Ram; the status-conscious King of Diamonds with the high-climbing Capricorn Goat; the judgmental King of Spades with the fair and balanced sign of Libra the Scales; and finally the genial and loving King of Hearts with the loyal, caring sign of Cancer the Crab.

In terms of numerology, the Kings are connected to unlucky Thirteen. Traditionally this has been (and still is) considered to be symbolic of misfortune, illness, death, and the intrusion of harsh reality. It is this last that is most telling—because in essence, the number does not express misfortune at all, but a shattering of illusions and the breakdown of stifling patterns of the past. Undoubtedly this is an uncomfortable process, but new situations replace the old and renewed optimism overwhelms mediocrity.

It has also been suggested that Thirteen is the number of leadership. Jesus led his twelve disciples, making their company thirteen in all. In legend, King Arthur presided over the twelve Knights of the Round Table, just as Robin Hood did with his merry men. This last example has a traditional affinity with British witchcraft, where covens of thirteen were said to be the ideal.

Each of the court cards is linked to a sign of the zodiac and the time of year that the sign encompasses. These date-sensitive cards may help you to work out approximately when something will occur, or when a problem will be resolved.

The King of Clubs

"Here comes the King of Clubs and shows
Thou hast some friends as well as foes;
Maids that do draw this card shall
Have very few, or none at all."

Traditional Name: This King is traditionally linked with one of the greatest rulers of the ancient world, Alexander II of Macedonia, better known as Alexander the Great (356–323 B.C.). Alexander inherited the throne of his mountainous kingdom and power over Greece when he was nineteen. He took on the vast Persian Empire and was declared a god and the son of the Egyptian deity, Ammon. Alexander went on to conquer the Person Empire as far as India, and many cities have been named after him.

Appearance: The King of Clubs has a ruddy complexion and a robust physique. He often has rich brown or red hair and hazel eyes. He has an energetic and lively personality.

Astrological Relationship: Like Ammon, this King is associated with the sign of the Ram or Aries (March 20 to April 20).

Meaning: The King of Clubs is a helpful friend upon whom the questioner can rely. If it is one of the first three cards drawn, and if the questioner is male, it is likely to represent him, but if the questioner is female this will denote an important man in her life. If elsewhere in the spread, this may indicate a work colleague or professional person who can give advice and help.

It is quite difficult to get to know the King of Clubs. He has been emotionally wounded in the past, so he has developed defensive barriers to prevent it from happening again. He has wide interests, and he is happy to socialize or to be left alone. He may be somewhat lonely, and he will only find happiness with a supportive partner who may not fully understand him yet who would not change him for the world.

Lenormand Number and Symbol: 6; Clouds.

The King of Diamonds

*"This noble King of Diamonds shows
Thou long shalt live where pleasure flows;
But when a woman draws the king,
Sad, melancholy songs she'll sing."*

Traditional Name: The King of Diamonds is traditionally shown in profile, like Roman emperors on coins, because this King is associated with Julius Caesar (100–44 B.C.), who was a cunning politician, great general, dictator, and unofficial emperor of Rome. The conqueror of Gaul, the first Roman invader of Britain, and lover of Queen Cleopatra, Julius Caesar dominated the ancient world. In a card reading, this King is associated with treason, but Caesar was also betrayed and slaughtered as a scapegoat.

Appearance: The King is thought of as a mature, distinguished man of military bearing. He has light or gray hair that may be thinning and cool blue or gray eyes. He has an air of confidence and authority.

Astrological Relationship: Ambitious and a scapegoat, this King is associated with Capricorn the Goat (December 23 to January 19).

Meaning: The King of Diamonds is sharp, perceptive, and shrewd, and he can quickly fathom the most complex issues. He can be impatient and demanding, and is always on the lookout for new territories to conquer. He may be a businessman, salesman, or tycoon. He would be a policy maker rather than a worker. Underneath his air of confidence, he is not so self-assured, and he can harbor self-doubt. He is vain and feels hurt if his pride is even mildly wounded. This King is loyal to those within his circle, but he can be dismissive of those who he neither likes nor respects. Some card readers see him as amoral or treacherous.

This card urges the questioner to take care in business dealings and to be patient in speculative ventures. If this is among the first three cards dealt, it refers to the questioner or to someone close by.

Lenormand Number and Symbol: 34; Fish.

The King of Spades

"By this brave king observe and note,
On golden streams you e'er shall float;
But women, by the selfsame lot,
Shall long enjoy what they have got."

Traditional Name: Many versions of this card show the King of Spades with a stylized harp, so he depicts the Biblical King David who was as at home with music as the sword as he was composing the psalms. He is sometimes identified as the illicit lover of Bathsheba. In the Middle Ages, this King was counted among the "Worthies." In divination, he is seen as a judge.

Appearance: This King is usually thought of as having dark hair and eyes and a sallow complexion. He has an air of authority and a forceful character.

Astrological Relationship: The King of Spades is associated with the Scales of Justice and thus with the sign of Libra (September 24 to October 23).

Meaning: The King of Spades is very sharp, witty, and intelligent. He has a strong will and is not above imposing it on other people. It is fortunate that he tends to be honest, truthful, and above board in his dealings. He may be an older man or one who is mature beyond his years. He relies on logic rather than intuition, and he may be out of touch with his feelings, or he may find it hard to express them. He sees things in terms of black and white or right and wrong. He may accuse those whose views are different from his of stupidity or obstinacy. His high principles can cost him dearly in terms of relationships.

If this is the first of three cards dealt for a male, it may represent the questioner or someone close by. For a female, this King symbolizes someone who has had a powerful influence on her for some time past.

Lenormand Number and Symbol: 30; Lilies.

The King of Hearts

"By this card surely 'twill appear
Thou shalt live long in happy cheer;
And if a woman draw this card,
She shall likewise be high preferred."

Traditional Name: The King of Hearts represents the only bona fide emperor in the deck, as he depicts Charles the Great, better known as Charlemagne (747–814 A.D.). Charlemagne was the King of the Franks and founder of the Holy Roman Empire. He is considered to be the founder of both France and Germany. Charlemagne had a company of knights called the Paladins (two of whom link with the Jacks of Diamonds and Spades). After his death, Charlemagne was declared a saint and became one of the "Worthies" in a deck of cards. He is given the name of the "Suicide King" due to his sad expression and the position of the sword on the card.

Appearance: The King has fair, auburn, or light-brown hair and blue, gray, or hazel eyes. He is friendly, open, and warm.

Astrological Relationship: This King links with Cancer the Crab (June 23 to July 23).

Meaning: Tradition says the King of Hearts is an older man due to his mature outlook and the humor with which he treats problems. Physical age is not the issue though, because this King expresses a wealth of experience, which may have been gained at a relatively young age. The King can represent the questioner if it is among the first three cards drawn, or it can represent the relative of a male or female questioner.

The King of Hearts represents a person with a strong character. He is fair-minded, genial, reliable, and open to new ideas. He is very emotional, but he may try to conceal this beneath a cool, gruff or forbidding exterior. He laughs a lot and cannot be serious for too long. He enjoys company and people, he likes humanity, and he is fun to be around. He can become sad and gloomy, but he soon perks up again.

Lenormand Number and Symbol: 4; House.

16

The Joker

It is commonly believed that the Joker is a vestige of the Major Arcana of the Tarot, and a direct descendant of the unnumbered Fool card. Alas, this is not so. The Joker was actually invented in 1857 as an addition to a standard deck of playing cards in the United States. Its original use was as the highest trump card in the game of Euchre. In divination, the Joker is optional, as it can stand as a chaotic influence that does not fit within the definitions of the four suits.

Meaning: The basic interpretation is of independence, unconventionality, and a need for personal freedom. When the Joker appears, it suggests that it is folly to believe that one can control all the events of one's life or truly predict the outcome of one's actions. It also implies the abandonment of fear and a readiness to explore unknown territory. The card is completely devoid of materialism and it may suggest that the practical values of life are no longer sufficient to fill the void in the questioner's soul.

The card can indicate the start of a spiritual quest or an inward journey; it can also indicate a literal journey of discovery or a change of life, leading to the unknown. It can warn against being a fool and advise the questioner to take care of his own interests.

If the Joker appears early in a reading or in a position suggesting the questioner, it denotes a spiritually evolved person who is somewhat at odds with his surroundings. The Joker is not petty, small-minded, greedy, or jealous—he follows his heart.

17

Telling Fortunes the Romany Way

In addition to reading a full deck of 52 cards, we should remember that there is a related tradition of reading a reduced pack of 32 cards, which seems to originate from the works of Etteilla. This manner of reading cards is used extensively by the Romany people (the gypsies) and it has become popular in Italy, France, and Germany. This may be because the game of Skat (which has been described as the national game of Germany) uses a reduced deck of cards.

Only the highest scoring cards are used, namely the Aces, Kings, Queens, Jacks, Tens, Nines, Eights, and Sevens. A variation that is likely to be familiar to Tarot readers is the use of reversed cards. This was once much easier than it is today, because until the mid-Nineteenth century all cards were "one-ended" much like Tarot cards are. In other words, the royal figures on the picture cards had feet! If you wish to use the 32 card methods, divide up a deck of cards and keep them strictly for the purpose of this method of divination. You will also have to mark your cards so that you can tell up from down, as it were. Your marks should be made before the pack is used.

Because so few cards are used in this form of divination, combinations of cards take on an extra importance in this system. I have listed the important card combinations immediately after giving the meanings of the individual cards.

The Suits

The general meanings of the suits are very close to those given to the normal poker deck.

Clubs are considered a very lucky suit connected with ambition and worldly success.

Diamonds are usually representative of financial affairs, material wealth, and possessions.

Spades deal with the grimmer aspects of life. Here we find losses and anxieties, illness and heartache. Spades are also linked to the emotions, disappointments in love, and feelings of regret.

Hearts are concerned with love and emotional life, but they are also associated with gains, domestic arrangements, and with socializing.

Clubs

Ace of Clubs
Upright: A very good card, suggesting health, wealth, and happiness. Letters and legal affairs will help bring good fortune. This may indicate a new business or the establishment of a happy partnership. If this is found with the Sevens of Diamonds and Clubs, great prosperity is forecast.

Reversed: Fortunes will slow down and there will be a delay in plans, or other bad news may turn up, but luck in love may offset this disappointment.

King of Clubs
Upright: A good friend who is influential, honorable and well-inclined towards the questioner. This person is quite sentimental, warmhearted, and straightforward. He hates underhanded dealings, and he is a faithful husband and companion.

Reversed: This man has good intentions, but he cannot seem to carry them through to a successful conclusion. He may be frustrated and plagued with thoughts of past failures. A happy countenance may mask inner sadness.

Queen of Clubs

Upright: A responsible woman who is up for a challenge. If this Queen is seen close to a male card, then she is a wife, partner, or close confidante. If this card is placed close by another Queen, the second Queen may be a rival; but she is honorable and somewhat in sympathy with the questioner.

Reversed: A greedy woman, faithless by nature, who puts her own interests first.

Jack of Clubs

Upright: A young, enterprising person who shows talent and promise. He is a dependable friend and faithful lover.

Reversed: This is a skillful and insincere flatterer who is also deceitful and dangerous.

Ten of Clubs

Upright: This card denotes luxury and prosperity, a holiday, or a pleasurable journey. However, these good things could be delayed by the presence of the Nine of Diamonds, or even completely ruined if beside the dreadful Nine of Spades.

Reversed: This represents a journey, possibly even an urgent flight from trouble. The reverse of this card hints at troublesome lawsuits and run-ins with authority.

Nine of Clubs

Upright: This is a very good indicator of a happy and fulfilling love life. If the questioner is single, it shows that romance is not far away, even if the questioner is skeptical about it. The card may also hint at an important gift, an unexpected windfall, or legacy.

Reversed: The reversed meaning is little different from the upright version, but it is on a smaller scale. It might indicate a light romance or a new friendship. A small but meaningful gift is also indicated.

Eight of Clubs

Upright: This is an ambivalent card, as it is good for affairs of the heart, but it has worrying implications concerning money. It can show the love of a person with a dark complexion or hair. It can also indicate a desperate desire for money.

Reversed: Unwise actions will cause a lot of trouble. In romantic affairs, it could show an infatuation with an unworthy person. In business, there is a strong possibility of underhanded dealings and the very real danger of gambling everything and losing.

Seven of Clubs

Upright: This card hints at youth and inexperience; of feelings that may be deep and intense but that also cause anxiety. In the same vein, the Seven of Clubs can indicate children, or in a wider sense, playfulness. This also shows the repayment of a debt and the establishment of goodwill.

Reversed: Small problems cause hiccups in relationships. Minor matters seem overly important.

Diamonds

Ace of Diamonds

Upright: A very important message or gift that will bring great personal satisfaction.

Reversed: This indicates an important communication that places extra responsibility on the questioner's shoulders.

King of Diamonds

Upright: The King of Diamonds is a distinguished man of military bearing, and he may have been in the armed forces or have worn some other kind of uniform. He is a person of great experience who generally knows what he is talking about. He can be helpful when he is in the right mood, but he is frequently preoccupied and self-absorbed.

Reversed: This denotes a schemer who betrays even his own plans, and he gives his intentions away before he can do any serious harm. If the reversed King of Diamonds is followed by his Queen, then a quarrelsome and unhappy marriage is shown.

Queen of Diamonds

Upright: A strong willed woman who is direct in speech and who always wants her own way. She may be prone to jealousy and she may interfere in other people's lives. Nevertheless, her influence is likely to be good.

Reversed: The above interpretation still holds true when the card is reversed, but her influence may tend to be bad.

Jack of Diamonds

Upright: Usually represents a reliable person who occupies an official position. The questioner may be able to do him a service that will win his gratitude.

Reversed: This is an opinionated person full of self-importance. He is a troublemaker and swindler.

Ten of Diamonds

Upright: This is a good card often indicating marriage, the establishment of a long and happy relationship, or a move to more congenial surroundings. Money luck and an excellent financial future are also shown.

Reversed: The reversed meaning has the opposite implication to the upright. There is still a move or a marriage, but in both cases it is ill advised. Financial losses are also indicated.

Nine of Diamonds

Upright: This is a frustrating card signifying delays and hindrances to plans. However, these irritations will eventually pass and may indeed prove to be blessings in disguise, saving the questioner from making a costly error.

Reversed: The reversed Nine shows problems in love and disagreements with a partner. The root of the quarrel is likely to be money.

Eight of Diamonds

Upright: This is one of the few "pip" cards that can indicate a person. In this case, it would signify a young professional or "merchant" who is important to the questioner's fortunes. However, it is more likely that the card means love letters or at least pleasing communications of an affectionate nature.

Reversed: This denotes disappointments in love, blighted hopes, and regret for that which will never be.

Seven of Diamonds

Upright: Communication in a social setting and idle chatter that is amusing but not to be taken too seriously. The questioner may receive some surprising news, but there is always the suspicion that it is only gossip. If the Seven of Diamonds is found with the Ace of Diamonds, then the questioner can expect really good news that is founded in fact.

Reversed: Criticism that is too harsh or unpleasant to hear. Issues involving children or pets could be hurtful or they may lead to misunderstandings.

Spades

Ace of Spades

Upright: Loss, grief, and sorrow of many kinds. If found with the Nine and Ten of Spades, news of a death. If the card stands alone, there will be bad news of another kind, possibly legal troubles, robbery, or betrayal.

Reversed: This warns of false friends, unwise speculation, treachery, and unwelcome news, possibly regarding injury or death.

King of Spades

Upright: A cold, hard, unforgiving man – possibly a widower or divorcé. He is a difficult man to get along with, and he could be a dangerous and vindictive enemy if provoked. On the other hand, if involved in a question of romance, the King of Spades is reliable and trustworthy. The card may also represent a person of social prestige such as a lawyer, judge, or doctor.

Reversed: All the negative traits of the upright King are trebled when the card is reversed. This is a dangerous and unscrupulous man. Legal losses can also be indicated.

Queen of Spades

Upright: Often a widow, divorcée, spinster, or a disappointed woman. This card also has a dark side, which can reveal a spiteful, cruel person who is an insincere friend—in reality, an enemy.

Reversed: This signifies a woman who is anxious to marry in spite of objections from friends and family. She may wed secretly.

Jack of Spades

Upright: A rude, rough, or ill-mannered person, although he can be intelligent and learned. This extremely eloquent critic could be a good friend as long as the questioner can overlook his faults.

Reversed: This is someone who is too friendly—he may be a deceitful and two-faced person who is not to be trusted.

Ten of Spades

Upright: This is a truly dreadful card signifying a string of disasters of one sort or another. It presages a succession of troubles that leaves the questioner feeling isolated and persecuted. Traditional interpretations stress grief, illness, or the loss of freedom. In short, the Ten of Spades deserves its rotten reputation as the worst card in the deck.

Reversed: It wouldn't be possible for the reversed Ten of Spades to be any worse than the upright meaning, so there is no additional information to add to that barrel-load of woes. Let us hope that the Nine or Ten of Hearts is not too far away, as this will provide an alleviation of at least some of the troubles.

Nine of Spades

Upright: This card brings bad news. Some information that the questioner receives will be very disturbing indeed. Tradition identifies the Nine of Spades with news of a death or illness, but it could just as easily indicate soaring anxiety and stress about the state of a relationship or business matter.

Reversed: If the upright meaning were not bad enough, the reversed position makes the situation even worse. Take a deep breath. Tell the questioner to be courageous and to always remember that even the worst of times do not last forever.

Eight of Spades

Upright: This card provides a health warning! It advises the questioner that unless he changes his ways and looks after himself then illness will surely follow. It may indicate the arrival of a person bearing bad news. This is emphasized if it is followed by the Seven of Diamonds. If a picture card is near, then there is the possibility of loss of employment and poverty.

Reversed: This signifies a rejected proposal or the casting aside of a relationship.

Seven of Spades

Upright: All Spades indicate anxiety, and the Seven is no different to the trend. In this case, the problem lies with imaginary fears and nightmares. The chances are that none of these bad things will become reality, but that does little to persuade the worrier that his fears are groundless.

Reversed: Indecision or the formulation of silly strategies, which would be seen to be foolish if only one had a clear head! Take sober advice and above all, remember the old saying, "When in doubt, do nowt [nothing]."

Hearts

Ace of Hearts

Upright: Good news, especially about romantic prospects. This indicates happy surroundings and a loving companion. If accompanied by picture cards, celebrations are in the offing, through marriage, joy, and good and fulfilling friendships.

Reversed: This can mean unexpected visitors or unsettling news. It might also point toward a change of home.

King of Hearts

Upright: The genial King of Hearts represents a wealthy man who loves the good life. He is generous to his friends and he is an excellent confidant and advisor. He is broad-minded and he has a good sense of humor, so the King of Hearts is by no means the "suicide king," which is his unkind nickname. His love of food and drink means that he is often portly, a fact that adds to rather than detracts from his distinguished looks.

Reversed: This king is not so genial when he is reversed. In fact he can be mean-spirited, stingy, and bombastic. He literally and metaphorically throws his weight around while hoping to hide his own timidity behind an aggressive front. He is great at making promises, but he is unlikely to keep a single one of them.

Queen of Hearts

Upright: For a man, this card means his true love. For a woman it signifies an unknown rival. More generally it reveals an open and honest woman who is obliging and caring.

Reversed: This implies obstacles to marriage or to the consummation of a love affair.

Jack of Hearts

Upright: This represents a carefree and happy person who is good to be with. The card hints at romance, especially for the young and single.

Reversed: It is time to mend a quarrel, patch up broken relationships, and declare an end to antagonism. This card may indicate someone in the military or in another kind of uniform.

Ten of Hearts

Upright: This is a card of happy surprises or of an unexpected rescue from troubles. Even if the questioner's woes are few, the appearance of the Ten of Hearts will bring even greater joy into his life. It may indicate moving on to something much better—possibly a long and enjoyable journey in the company of someone the enquirer loves.

Reversed: There is no negative influence in this card, so it has no reversed meaning in the strict sense. However, as is the case with most of the positive cards, when reversed it may indicate the delay of perfect happiness for a while.

Nine of Hearts

Upright: This is the "wish card" that suggests that one of the questioner's fondest desires is about to come true. Happiness and contentment will surround him. It may indicate celebrations and enjoyable events that are already planned and of which he is already aware, or an amazing and wonderful surprise. The most fortunate aspect of this card is that if the reading is full of doom and gloom, the Nine of Hearts can alleviate suffering and will often provide an antidote to these troubles.

Reversed: A short period of sorrow will be swept away completely by the happy times that immediately follow it.

Eight of Hearts

Upright: This card is very good news for those who like a quiet, orderly life. It does not foretell great excitement, just a happy, humdrum existence where everything fits into place with no trouble. As a card of advice, it promotes the virtues of humility and moderation in all things. The card may also show the affections of a pale or fair-haired person.

Reversed: The questioner may feel offended by the unresponsiveness of someone he desires.

Seven of Hearts

Upright: The traditional meaning of this card is marriage. Furthermore, it states that if the questioner is a woman, her future offspring will be girls. If the questioner is male, then he is destined for a happy and prosperous future. Modern interpretations emphasize making the right choices, wisdom, and competence in both affairs of the heart and in more practical endeavors.

Reversed: This denotes a need for recognition or fame, and if this is not forthcoming then boredom and despondency will set in. It may indicate a passionate relationship that is marred by jealousy.

Combinations of Cards of the Same Value

Four Aces
Four aces together are ominous, and they imply danger. Financial losses are possible, as are a host of other troubles such as an emotional rift or even confinement of some kind. The more reversed Aces there are, the better, because this is a sign that at least some of the harm will be undone.

Three Aces
These indicate a time of trouble that will eventually be relieved by good news. Three Aces may show a faithless lover. If the Aces are reversed, then the questioner should mind his behavior, because he is prone to foolish excesses.

Two Aces
This means coming together. If the Aces are Hearts and Clubs, it is all to the good, as the questioner will benefit. If they are Diamonds and Spades, then he is likely to suffer from an unholy union. If one or both are reversed, the outlook is bleak.

Four Kings
This is an excellent indication of advancement, success, the respect of one's peers, and a well-deserved honor. If all the Kings are reversed, the gains will have less value, but they will arrive sooner.

Three Kings
Serious and pressing matters will be dealt with swiftly and efficiently. Should any of the Kings be reversed, then there are hidden complexities that will take time to sort out. If all three are

reversed, the questioner should seek another avenue for his talents because this one will get him nowhere.

Two Kings

This represents a good business partnership, cooperation, and honest dealings. Each reversed King represents an obstacle that can be overcome with effort.

Four Queens

This denotes a social gathering that may be spoiled if any of the Queens are reversed.

Three Queens

This indicates friendly visitors who bring good news. If all of the Queens are reversed, there will be gossip, scandal, and a threat to the questioner's interests.

Two Queens

This symbolizes a meeting between friends during which confidences are exchanged. If either Queen is reversed, a rivalry exists and it is likely that a secret will be betrayed. If both Queens are reversed, then the questioner will suffer as the result of his own actions.

Four Jacks

Youthful exuberance, a lot of fun, but perhaps overindulgence leading to petty arguments. The more inverted Jacks there are the better.

Three Jacks

This indicates treachery and false friends. Again, inverted cards are good news, as they undo the work of troublemakers.

Two Jacks

This is only important if the Jacks happen to be Hearts and Clubs. The Jack of Hearts is said to loathe the Jack of Clubs, so if these two are found together then the questioner can expect trouble. A very old interpretation of two Jacks is a duel.

Three Tens

Wealth, good fortune, success in whatever venture the questioner is undertaking. Each reversed Ten represents an obstacle that can be overcome with persistence.

Two Tens

This suggests lawsuits and legal problems. If either or both Tens are reversed, there is more chance of a ruling in the enquirer's favor. If the two Tens are red ones, then a wedding or celebration is in the offing.

Four Nines

This denotes a happy surprise or an unexpected event. The number of reversed nines represents the time period before the surprise occurs.

Three Nines

This one is a superb omen of health, wealth, and happiness. If all the Nines are reversed, it is still good, although the questioner will have to go through some temporary financial problems before the blessings flow his way.

Two Nines

Contentment in personal life and the success of a business venture. This may also indicate a change of address. If the cards happen to be the Nine of Clubs and Nine of Hearts, an inheritance is indicated. Should either or both Nines be reversed, then there are minor worries but still this remains a good combination.

Four Eights

This is a "swings and roundabouts" sort of combination. The questioner will win through in some areas only to find that he has lost in others. It is better if all the Eights are reversed, because the picture becomes far more stable, and this will do wonders for the questioner's personal stress levels.

Three Eights

This is a sign of marriage, a strong emotional commitment, or the birth of a child. When all the Eights are reversed, it is an omen of debauchery, foolishness, and self-indulgence.

Two Eights

This indicates infatuations, flirtations, and pleasant surprises. If both Eights are reversed, there will be unpleasant developments in the love life. The Eight of Diamonds with the Eight of Hearts signifies a journey and also new buying clothes in readiness for a celebration. The Eight of Diamonds with Eight of Spades represents sickness. The Eight of Diamonds with Eight of Clubs brings deep and lasting love.

Four Sevens

This denotes cunning schemes and worrying pitfalls that are likely to arise from envy. If all Sevens are reversed, then the questioner's enemies may wound him, but they are powerless to do any lasting damage.

Three Sevens

This is a sad combination foretelling the loss of friends, regret, and possibly also guilt. When reversed, the three Sevens are reminiscent of a hangover or some other unpleasant reaction to a time of pleasure.

Two Sevens

This suggests a welcome surprise, a happy event, and the development of deep, lasting, mutual love. If both Sevens are reversed, it is not as good as it indicates infidelity, remorse, and guilt.

Various Card Combinations and Interpretations

Ten of Diamonds with Seven of Spades
Delays and frustrations.

Ten of Diamonds with Eight of Clubs
A journey prompted by love.

Seven of Diamonds with Queen of Diamonds
Important decisions and ambitious efforts.

Ten of Clubs with an Ace
*A large sum of money. If these are followed by an Eight and a
King, a marriage proposal.*

The Nine, Ace, and Ten of Diamonds
*Important news from a distance. If followed by a court card, then a
journey will be necessary.*

Eight and Seven of Diamonds
Gossip and scandal will be traced back to its source.

King, Queen and Ace of one color
*A sign of romance and marriage. If the Queen or Jack of Spades is
present, then there will be family objections and difficulties. The
proximity of the Eight of Spades foretells misfortune, but happiness
is assured if the Eight of Hearts or Clubs appear.*

Ace of Diamonds and Ten of Hearts
Marriage, happiness, celebrations, joy.

Seven of Spades with a Court card
A false friend.

A sequence of Spades
Jealousy, malice, despondency, money losses.

King of Hearts and Nine of Hearts
An excellent omen for lovers.

Queen and Jack of Spades
A hostile, malicious influence is at work.

A sequence of Court cards
Festivities, hospitality and good companions.

A Court card placed between two cards of the same number
An element of threat, as if the central card is being menaced in some way. This combination often shows a confrontation with authority.

18

Romany Card Deck Spreads

All the spreads in this section are traditional ones. They are well over a century old and some may be even older. As usual for a card reading, a calm, receptive frame of mind is the first requirement.

Take the 32-card Romany Deck and shuffle it thoroughly, remembering to turn some cards around to provide reversed meanings. The questioner cuts the deck (traditionally with the left hand) and gives it back to the reader, who then arranges the cards according to one of these ancient patterns. The reader goes through a complex preliminary activity of cutting and dividing the cards before the reading begins. This fiddling around has a useful purpose, in that it takes both the reader and the questioner away from daily life activities and encourages them to slip into a meditative and receptive frame of mind.

The Past, Present, and Future Spread

This method of card reading is at least 200 years old. It has been used widely in Europe and among the gypsies all over the world.

The 32-card deck is shuffled and cut in the usual way. After this, the two piles are not put back together until the top card of one and the bottom card of the other have been put aside. These two cards remain outside the reading. The reader then deals the remaining 30 cards into three equal piles, each of which contains ten cards. These cards are laid out in three horizontal lines from left to right. The ten cards at the top represent the past, the middle row is the present, and bottom row shows the future.

The first consideration is to take note of the card groups in each of the three rows and to interpret these to give a background to

☐ ☐ ☐ ☐ ☐ ☐ ☐ ☐ ☐ ☐

☐ ☐ ☐ ☐ ☐ ☐ ☐ ☐ ☐ ☐

☐ ☐ ☐ ☐ ☐ ☐ ☐ ☐ ☐ ☐

the reading. After this, it is a matter of interpreting each card in turn and weaving a story by linking each card in the sequence to its predecessor.

Example

In this case, the questioner is a fair-haired young man, so the Jack of Hearts is a suitable card for him. After shuffling and cutting, the cards were as follows:

Past: Queen of Clubs, King of Diamonds, Ten of Clubs, Nine of Diamonds, Eight of Clubs, Ace of Diamonds, Ace of Hearts, Jack of Spades, Queen of Spades, and Eight of Diamonds.

Present: Ace of Spades, Seven of Diamonds, Eight of Hearts, Queen of Hearts, Seven of Hearts, Queen of Diamonds, Nine of Spades, King of Hearts, Jack of Hearts, and Ten of Diamonds.

Future: Jack of Diamonds, Seven of Clubs, Eight of Spades, Seven of Spades, Ten of Spades, Nine of Hearts, King of Clubs, Ten of Hearts, King of Spades, and Ace of Spades.

When looking at the cards that represent the past, we notice that there are three pairs. There are two Queens, both of which are reversed. This suggests that the questioner is suffering from the consequences of his own actions. The two Aces speak of good intentions and the start of a partnership or relationship—but both of these cards are reversed, which is not a good sign. The two Eights tell of pleasure-seeking and perhaps hint at frivolous love affairs.

Taken in sequence, the cards show the following: A possessive woman (Queen of Clubs) and a schemer (King of Diamonds). The Ten of Clubs denotes a journey that did not go well, as emphasized by the Nine of Diamonds. The Eight of Clubs refers to the thoughts and affections of a dark woman (probably the Queen of Clubs). The Ace of Diamonds represents worrying news, probably concerning property, as depicted by the reversed Ace of Hearts. The Jack of Spades symbolizes an untrustworthy person who might have legal or official connections. The Queen of Spades refers to a recently divorced woman.

It appears that this young man's past has been filled with emotional confusion. Although he had the full intention of committing himself to a relationship, there was too much jealousy and intrigue surrounding it for it to work. With so many cards indicating untrustworthy people, there was also a good chance of malicious gossip surrounding the situation.

In the present there are two pairs. There are two Sevens, which hint at mutual affection and two Queens (one of whom is reversed) suggesting a rivalry.

In sequence, the cards reveal that the Ace of Spades is sweeping away the past. This kind of thing is traumatic, but our questioner receives little sympathy or understanding due to the presence of the Seven of Diamonds. The Eight of Hearts shows him considering commitment (even marriage) to the Queen of Hearts—but the Seven of Hearts also denotes that he will achieve a sense of contentment that he will be reluctant to change. To prove that old amorous habits die hard, there seems to be a link with the Queen of Diamonds, and she is not above using emotional blackmail to keep him. The Nine of Spades shows us that this relationship is harmful. Many promises are made but none are kept—as shown by the reversed King of Hearts. The next card is the questioner's own, the reversed Jack of Hearts. This suggests that the questioner is a little battered and disappointed and that he would like to patch up quarrels and mend broken relationships. There may be a good chance of this because the Ten of Diamonds can indicate the establishment of a long and happy relationship. This also hints at a move to new and more congenial surroundings.

For the future segment of the reading, the card combinations include Four of Spades, which looks like trouble. There are a couple of Sevens, one of which is reversed, so there is mutual affection but also some possibility of deceit. The two Tens point to good luck, even though one of them is the Ten of Spades. The two Kings suggest cooperation and a good partnership.

Our questioner is now shown as the Jack of Diamonds reversed, so he is revealed as being opinionated. The Seven of Clubs talks of youth and inexperience and suggests that he learn from the events in his troubled love life and then move on. The Eight of Spades reversed symbolizes a rejected proposal, while the Seven of the same suit emphasizes his emotional confusion.

The gloom continues with Ten of Spades, because he will feel isolated and persecuted. However, there is a ray of hope indicated by the Nine of Hearts, which is the wish card, showing that one of his fondest desires is about to come true. This is due to the influence of a good friend, the King of Clubs. The Ten of Hearts follows with a happy surprise and an unexpected rescue from the questioner's troubles. There still remains some resentment, because the King of Spades represents unforgiving attitudes. However, if this is a question of romance, the outlook is better—because this King is said to forecast stable, long-lasting relationships.

The last card is the reversed Ace of Clubs, showing that our questioner—the originally happy-go-lucky Jack of Hearts—still has a lot to learn, but nevertheless, he still seems to cast a spell over the ladies!

The French Method

The Romany deck of 32 cards is shuffled and cut in the usual way. The reader then deals the cards into two equal packs comprising sixteen cards each. The questioner then chooses one of the packs. The first card is taken from the top of this pack and put aside face downward to provide the "surprise." The remaining fifteen cards are then turned face upwards in order from left to right. If the significator, which is the card chosen to represent the questioner, is not among these cards then the reading must be abandoned and started all over again.

The reader then looks for card groupings, which may be two of a kind, three of a kind, or four of a kind such as three Aces, four Kings, etc. These are then interpreted according to the rules of card combinations (see the relevant chapter).

The next step is to start with the significator and then count seven cards along to find the next card in the sequence. Count seven more on from that card, returning to the start of the row if necessary, and continue until you return to a card that you have already interpreted.

Thirdly, the reader interprets the first and last cards that were initially dealt in order to end this part of the reading.

Example

The questioner is a tall, dark-haired young man who at the time of the reading was in search of a job. The card chosen to represent him was the Jack of Clubs.

After shuffling and cutting he chose the left-hand pack and the deal was as follows:

Nine of Hearts, Queen of Spades, Seven of Spades, Seven of Diamonds, Seven of Clubs, Ten of Spades, Ace of Spades, Queen of Hearts, Jack of Clubs, Queen of Clubs, King of Spades, Ace of Hearts, Eight of Spades, Ten of Hearts, Nine of Spades.

Beginning at the significator (Jack of Clubs) and counting along seven cards, the proper sequence was found:

Jack of Clubs, Nine of Spades, Ace of Spades, Ten of Hearts, Ten of Spades, Eight of Spades, Seven of Clubs, Ace of Hearts, Seven of Diamonds, King of Spades, Seven of Spades, Queen of Clubs, Queen of Spades.

The next count brings us back to the position of Jack of Clubs, so we end there.

The card combinations reveal that there are two Queens, two tens, and three sevens. The predominant suit is Spades.

Two Queens speak of a rivalry between friends (because one of them is reversed). The two Tens reveal possible problems concerning legal matters and contracts. The three Sevens indicate feelings of guilt and the possible loss of friends. However, none of the Sevens are reversed so this may indicate a temporary situation. The Spades suit deals with anxieties and losses as well as heartache. This person may have recently faced a disappointment. A King, Queen, and Ace of the same color are present, and this signifies happiness and the formation of strong emotional links, so the news is not all bad. It is fortunate that the Spades are not in a continuous sequence; otherwise malice, jealousy, and money losses would be indicated.

Taking the cards individually, our questioner (the Jack of Clubs) has been faced with some bad news, which has added to his level of stress. He may be worried about his chances of finding suitable employment. He certainly feels sorrow and a sense of loss as revealed by the reversed Ace of Spades, but the Ten of Hearts brings a happy surprise that will lift him from a pit of gloom and help him to move on to something much better. The Ten of Spades comes next, and this shows that he will have to surrender some of his freedom to achieve this new, improved position.

The following card advises him to change his ways and to look after himself or he is likely to make himself ill. This warning is connected to his innate playfulness, as shown by Seven of Clubs. Perhaps the cards are telling him that a more mature attitude is now required. Romantically, things are looking up, as suggested by the Ace of Hearts. There is also the probability that he will move to more congenial surroundings where he will make good friends. This is emphasized by Seven of Diamonds, which indicates fun and an active social life. The reversed King of Spades shows that he has a mean and vindictive enemy, but this person seems to do no harm other than causing the questioner a little more anxiety (Seven of Spades). It is likely that jealousy is at the root of the problem (Queen of Clubs), but the cool common sense of the Queen of Spades will calm his fears. The Queen of Spades is likely to represent the questioner's mother.

The first and last cards from the initial deal are Nine of Hearts and Nine of Spades. Two Nines are an excellent omen, indicating a happy personal life and the success of a business venture. Individually the cards show a balance between optimism and pessimism, the Nine of Hearts being the "wish card" promising success, happiness, and fulfillment of desires, while the Nine of Spades says that, although this is true, it won't stop the questioner from worrying!

The French Method Continued...

The next step in the French method is to shuffle the fifteen cards once more, cut them, and deal them into three packs of five cards. The top card from each of the three packs is removed unseen and is placed with the card that has already been put aside as the "surprise," so that you are left with four packs of four cards each. The questioner must then choose one of the four piles, which will either represent his question or his immediate concerns. After this is interpreted, the questioner will choose another pile to represent his home, family, and general domestic circumstances. The third pile is then read. This represents new things entering the questioner's life. The pack containing the "surprise" is left until last and should provide the final details to round off the reading.

Example

The first pack reveals the questioner and his immediate concerns:

Ace of Hearts, Queen of Spades, Jack of Clubs, and Nine of Hearts.

The Ace of Hearts reveals that the questioner is an emotional person who is generally optimistic. He comes from happy surroundings. The card is immediately followed by two picture cards showing that a celebration will shortly follow as will the establishment of good, fulfilling friendships. The first picture card is Queen of Spades. This is a divorcée who does not fit the traditional interpretation of "Black Maria"; in fact, she is likely to represent the questioner's mother. The Jack of Clubs is next, and this depicts the questioner himself being close proximity to the "wish card," which is the Nine of Hearts. This indicates that his desires will come true and he will soon get that longed-for job. This is likely to come out of the blue.

The second pack reveals home and family issues:

Queen of Hearts, Ace of Spades, Seven of Clubs, and Eight of Spades.

The Queen of Hearts refers to the questioner's true love, but the Ace of Spades next to it indicates a loss. The reversed Seven of Clubs shows that this may only be a temporary hitch because minor matters are being blown out of all proportion. However this trend seems to continue, because the reversed Eight of Spades suggests a rejection.

The third pack reveals new things entering the questioner's life:

Ten of Hearts, Nine of Spades, Seven of Spades, and Ten of Spades.

The Ten of Hearts is always a good card, as it indicates a happy and surprising set of events that will lift the questioner's spirits. However, he is obviously a complex person, because the anxiety indicated by Nine of Spades immediately follows. The reversed Seven of Spades shows some indecision, but the Ten of Spades (commonly known as the worst card in the deck) means that this period of time is the lowest point in the questioner's fortunes and that from here the only way is up!

The fourth pack contains the "surprise," thus the unknown and future indications:

Queen of Clubs, King of Spades, Seven of Diamonds, and King of Clubs.

The surprise section of the reading begins with a warning concerning another person's jealousy and malice, as shown by the Queen of Clubs and King of Spades. This is the enemy that has been spoken of in the first part of the reading. The gender is not specified, but it is likely the person involved has dark hair. The Seven of Diamonds shows that a social venue is the arena for some surprising and possibly unpleasant news. However, a good friend in the shape of King of Clubs will be on hand to provide the questioner with emotional support.

The French Method Continued Further...

If this method is used in connection with a question of inheritance, the presence of the upright Ace of Spades is necessary to the reading as an indication of profit as the result of a death. It is a further indication of a considerable legacy if the Seven, Eight, Nine, or Ten of Clubs are found with the Ace.

In matters concerning lawsuits, the King of Spades is a necessary card within the reading. Should all the other major Spade cards also appear, the Queen, Jack, Ace, or Ten, then the judgment is likely to be bad, either because the questioner will lose the case or because it will bring him no profit. On the other hand, if the Ace of Spades is accompanied by all four Tens, then the chances of success are vastly improved.

To discover a thief, all four Jacks must appear. In addition to this, the presence of the King and the Eight of Spades means that the villain has already been apprehended. If the Ace of Spades also puts in an appearance, the prisoner is in danger of severe punishment. The Ace of Clubs, the King of Clubs, or the Queen of Hearts all hold out the hope that the thief will repent and compensate his victim. Finally, if there are more Diamonds in the reading than any other sort of card, then it is likely that the thief has already been arrested for some other crime.

The Italian Method

The Italian method has some similarities to the French method, and it would be a matter of heated debate as to which came first.

A deck of 32 cards is shuffled and cut as usual (remembering to turn some to provide reversed meanings). The reader then deals out the pack onto a table in a horizontal row, face upward, three cards at a time. Italian tradition tells us that the cards should be laid from the right to the left, using the left hand.

If three cards of the same suit are turned up at once, they are left in place and they form part of the reading. If two of the three cards of the same suit are dealt, only the higher value card is selected while the other is discarded. This process is continued until there are fifteen cards face upward on the table.

It is absolutely necessary that the significator is present. If this court card is not among the cards, then the reading should be abandoned. The cards should be mixed together again and the whole process of shuffling and cutting begun once more.

Assuming the significator is present, the next step is to count five cards along to the left to find the next card of the reading, then count five further cards to choose the next, and so on until you reach the end of the row. Continue again from the beginning and keep on counting until all fifteen all have been included. This order of cards gives the narrative and sense of time to the first part of the reading.

Example
The questioner is a fair-haired lady who runs her own business. She divorced a long time ago, but does not have any bitterness about it. The lady is very forthright, so the Queen of Diamonds rather than the Queen of Spades (a more traditional choice for a divorcée) has been chosen to represent her.

After shuffling and cutting, the 15 cards were dealt in the following order:

Seven of Diamonds, Queen of Hearts, King of Spades, Ten of Diamonds, Nine of Diamonds, Jack of Hearts, Ten of Hearts, Jack of Diamonds, Queen of Diamonds, Ace of Diamonds, Jack of Spades, Nine of Spades, King of Clubs, Ten of Spades, and Ace of Hearts.

Counting five from the significator we arrive at the Ten of Spades, five cards further on and we see the King of Spades, and so on. The order of the cards is now as follows:

Ten of Spades, Ten of Diamonds, Queen of Diamonds, Ace of Hearts, Nine of Diamonds, Ace of Diamonds, Seven of Diamonds, Jack of Hearts, Jack of Spades, Queen of Hearts, Ten of Hearts, Nine of Spades, King of Spades, Jack of Diamonds, and King of Clubs.

The above sequence yields no less than four pairs and two triplets. We have two Aces, two Kings, two Queens, and two Nines, as well as three Jacks and three Tens. The two Aces indicate that something is coming together, but this is not necessarily for the good because one of them is reversed. The two Kings emphasize this message because they concern partnerships, especially business partnerships. Neither King is reversed, so this is likely to be beneficial. The pair of Queens represents a meeting in which confidences are exchanged. The trio of Tens is a good omen symbolizing wealth and good fortune. However, one Ten is reversed, which represents an obstacle that can only be overcome by persistence. Finally, the three Jacks shout a warning against treachery and false friends. Fortunately the problem is not too serious, because two of the three Jacks are reversed.

In addition, the Seven of Diamonds found with the Queen of the same suit shows that there are important decisions to be made. The Ace, Nine, and Ten of Diamonds in the same row indicate important news from a distance, and the Queen of Diamonds suggests that a journey must soon follow.

The King, Queen, and Ace of Diamonds are present, which tells us that a marriage or firm commitment is planned. However, the presence of the Jack of Spades tells of objections and interference. Nevertheless, the Ace of Diamonds sitting with the Ten of Hearts shows that happiness will prevail and celebrations will follow.

The run of court cards at the end of the sequence indicates the company of people that the questioner respects and likes.

Taken individually, the cards begin badly—with the dreadful reversed Ten of Spades showing a time of great confusion, trouble, betrayal, and isolation. This is followed by Ten of Diamonds, which denotes better luck and a far better outlook both emotionally and financially. The significator (the Queen of Diamonds) follows, representing the questioner herself, and she is now looking forward to a more fun-filled romantic life. The Nine of Diamonds is problematic for her love life, as it shows some delays to her plans, but these are blessings in disguise. The reversed Ace of Diamonds that follows indicates extra responsibilities placed on the questioner's shoulders. There may be unjustified criticism due to the presence of the reversed Seven of Diamonds, and the possibility of new love owing to the reversed Jack of Hearts. However he is not all that he appears to be, so the questioner must take care. The Jack of Spades is another admirer, a professional person who may intelligent and dark, with smoldering looks. He may be rude and harsh to the questioner's opponents but will prove himself to be a good friend to her. The Queen of Hearts indicates that our questioner has a female rival who may be unknown to her, but this fact is unlikely to mar her happiness much since the joyful Ten of Hearts follows. Even so, she is likely to experience some anxiety due to the presence of the Nine of Spades, but the King of Spades suggests that a professional man will be on hand to offer her advice and guidance. This ending to the story is reinforced by Jack of Diamonds, who represents a reliable person who occupies an official position. Finally, there is the King of Clubs, who is a warmhearted and straightforward friend.

The last three picture cards are similar in meaning and may therefore represent further aspects of the people in question rather than even more characters on the scene.

To move on to the next part of the reading, shuffle the fifteen cards and deal them into five small piles of three cards each. These should be placed in a row from right to left.

> Pack 1 – The questioner.
> Pack 2 – Home, family and security.
> Pack 3 – Events that are unexpected.
> Pack 4 – Events that are expected.
> Pack 5 – The surprise.

A further card can now be taken from the unused discarded portion of the Romany deck. This card is called the "Consolation," because this card reveals the life lesson that can be learned from the reading.

Example:

Pack 1 – The questioner: Ace of Hearts, Queen of Diamonds, and Ace of Diamonds.
This pack shows the questioner to be a strong-willed woman who likes to have her own way. She may occasionally interfere in other people's business, although usually she has the best of motives. At the moment she feels somewhat threatened, because she sits between two cards of the same value. Fortunately these are Aces, suggesting a new bond, perhaps one that she does not feel quite ready to accept. Even so, there is an important communication (Ace of Diamonds) concerning the questioner's romantic prospects.

Pack 2 – Home, family, and security: Nine of Spades, Nine of Diamonds, and Ten of Hearts.
This lady's family is a source of anxiety (Nine of Spades) so family complications force her to delay her plans (Nine of Diamonds). This leads to frustration, but all these problems are put in perspective by the joyful Ten of Hearts, which shows an unexpected beneficial development that will alleviate her troubles. It is useful to note that two Nines denote contentment in one's personal life.

Pack 3 – Events that are unexpected: King of Spades, Seven of Diamonds, and King of Clubs.
Two Kings in this pile relate to the development of a partnership, and while this is usually something to do with business, it can also have some personal aspects. The questioner meets a reliable, trustworthy advisor (King of Spades) in a social setting (Seven of Diamonds). He will become a good and faithful friend and ally (King of Clubs).

Pack 4 – Events that are expected: Ten of Spades, Jack of Hearts, and Queen of Hearts.
Worry, worry, and more worry can be expected (Ten of Spades). This disquiet is caused—at least in part—by the reversed Jack of Hearts and his secret paramour, the Queen of Hearts. It is likely that this pair represent a lover—the questioner's rival—who appears to be a beautiful woman.

Pack 5 – The surprise: Ten of Diamonds, Jack of Spades, and Jack of Diamonds.
A marriage is shown by the Ten of Diamonds; however this is not likely to be with the fickle Jack of Hearts, but to someone who fulfills the qualities of the Jack of Spades and Jack of Diamonds— a reliable person who has good prospects and who occupies an official position of some kind. He may appear superficially uncouth but he is loyal and intelligent.

The Consolation: Ace of Clubs.
The life lesson that the questioner can learn from this experience is that she should establish a new partnership that will lead to a happy and fulfilled life. She should not be afraid of new influences and events coming into her life, or allow herself to be held back by misplaced loyalty to someone disloyal to her.

19

The Lenormand System

The Lenormand system is also known as the *Petit Lenormand* system. The first step is to take a new deck of cards and then discard the twos, threes, fours, and fives. There are no upright or reversed cards in this system, so you can write the name and number of the appropriate symbol on each card for ease of reference. These are listed in the following table. If you prefer, you can buy a Lenormand deck, usually easy to find via the Internet.

CARD SYMBOLISM AND NUMBERING							
	Clubs		**Diamonds**		**Spades**		**Hearts**
Ace	Ring	(25)	Sun	(31)	Lady	(29)	Man	(28)
King	Clouds	(6)	Fish	(34)	Lilies	(30)	House	(4)
Queen	Serpent	(7)	Roads	(22)	Flowers	(9)	Stork	(17)
Jack	Scourge	(11)	Scythe	(10)	Child	(13)	Heart	(24)
10	Bear	(15)	Book	(26)	Ship	(3)	Dog	(18)
9	Fox	(14)	Coffin	(8)	Anchor	(35)	Cavalier	(1)
8	Mountain	(21)	Key	(33)	Garden	(20)	Moon	(32)
7	Mouse	(23)	Birds	(12)	Letter	(27)	Tree	(5)
6	Cross	(36)	Clover	(2)	Tower	(19)	Stars	(16)

Marie Lenormand gave each card a unique interpretation, quite unlike any other form of card reading. It is tempting to speculate that she was influenced by Tarot, numerology, or some other form of occult lore such as the 36 decans of the zodiac in the construction of the card symbolism. However, I am inclined to believe that these symbols were more personal, and that they had deep significance to the life and experiences of Marie Lenormand herself.

The Meaning of the Cards

1   Nine of Hearts—Cavalier (Knight, Horseman)

This is the first card in the sequence, symbolized by a mounted cavalier, horseman, or knight. It suggests a favorable outlook to whatever question has been asked. According to Mlle. Lenormand herself, the Cavalier means good news given by a stranger from far away. It may also mean travel, excitement, and new things coming into the questioner's life.

2   Six of Diamonds—Clover

This card has the happy symbol of the clover or trefoil. Like the lucky shamrock, this is a card of good omen, so if it is found close to the significator then the questioner's present troubles will soon be swept away. Even if this card is surrounded by grim ones there is still a glimmer of luck to light the way. The clover also indicates speed, events which occur or pass away very quickly.

3   Ten of Spades—Ship

In total contrast to normal card-reading practice, this card is identified with a ship with golden sails, numbered with a lucky three in this system. The Ship brings opportunities because it sails into port with a cargo of good fortune. If it is found adjacent to the significator then a memorable journey is forecast.

4   King of Hearts—House

This card refers to a happy home and signifies that your aims will be successfully completed. However, if this card is in a central position in a reading and is found below the significator, then a cautious approach in dealing with one's neighbors is highly recommended.

5 *Seven of Hearts—Tree*

This card is symbolized as a great tree, the strength of which is reflected in its interpretation as an indicator of good health. If found close to the significator, the outlook is very favorable indeed, as it denotes that the questioner is not only protected but that his wishes are set to come true.

6 *King of Clubs—Clouds*

The King's meaning varies here. The clouds are light or dark and foreboding, depending on whether the card is to the right or left, above or below the significator. To the right or above, all will be well and life will be happily ordered; to the left or below, doubt and confusion reign and truth is obscured.

7 *Queen of Clubs—Serpent*

This was not one of Mlle. Lenormand's favorite cards. She connected it with the cunning serpent that lulls the questioner into a false sense of security before striking. The message is that the questioner should be wary of those in his company whom he does not know well. He should not be too ready to please or to follow another's lead and most of all to beware a flatterer.

8 *Nine of Diamonds—Coffin*

This card carries the grim symbolism of a coffin. As might be imagined, this card means sickness, sorrow, and loss. This need not refer to a person, but it is a sure indicator that something is gone from the questioner's life and that it should now be buried. The closer this card is to the significator, the worse its impact on the questioner's life.

9 *Queen of Spades—Flowers*

As is often the case, the view of Mlle. Lenormand, the meaning of this card is contrary to other traditions. She sees this Queen as a bouquet of flowers. In her view the card is encouraging, because it urges one to forget the sadness of past because happiness is just around the corner.

10   Jack of Diamonds—Scythe

In the strange symbolism of Mlle. Lenormand, the Jack of Diamonds is depicted as a scythe. This card means danger and that strangers are intent on harming the questioner. However, if the Jack is in close proximity to more positive cards then he will overcome opposition and malice.

11   Jack of Clubs—Birch Rod (Whip, Scourge)

Mlle. Lenormand gave this card the harsh symbol of a whip, scourge, or birch rod. She said categorically that the card meant marital strife, quarrels, and sorrow.

12   Seven of Diamonds—Birds

The deceptively simple image of birds takes the place of the Seven of Diamonds in the Lenormand system. Birds signify that any difficulties the questioner experiences will last only a very short time. Life may be less than perfect for a while, but the sacrifice will be worth it in the long term. If far from the significator, the birds reveal that the enquirer will have to make a journey very soon—probably unexpectedly.

13   Jack of Spades—Child

In contrast to the often-sinister interpretations of the Jack of Spades, Mlle. Lenormand chose to symbolize him as an innocent and loveable child. She associates the card with acts of kindness and new friendships—despite the fact she numbered the card unlucky 13.

14   Nine of Clubs—Fox

The Nine of Clubs is identified with a cunning and greedy Fox. If near the significator, it clearly shows that someone close to the questioner has a hidden agenda and is out to deceive. It warns of betrayal and urges the questioner to be extra vigilant. The farther from the significator it is, the more likely that the questioner will find himself in at least reasonably trustworthy company.

15   Ten of Clubs—Bear

According to this unique system, this is an ominous card called the bear. Fifteen is the number of the Devil card in the Tarot deck and some of its symbolism is quite similar. It shows trouble caused by envy, and it advises against being too trusting or revealing too many personal details.

16   Six of Hearts—Star(s)

The Six of Hearts is symbolized as a star or a clear starry night, and like its counterpart in the Tarot deck is a sign of hope, of gifts, good fortune, and a positive attitude. If the Star is surrounded by ominous cards, then the questioner will need to keep a positive attitude to help him wade his way through a succession of difficulties. Even so, there will be some progress and even minor gains. Generally speaking, this card promises that all will be well in the end.

17   Queen of Hearts—Stork

In the Lenormand system this card is symbolized by a stork, and this signifies travel. If it is to the left, or below the significator, this card can mean abandonment or that someone is distancing himself from the questioner. There may be reasons why this is not such a bad thing, but even so, the enquirer could possibly regain this person's allegiance if he is prepared to put the effort into doing so.

18   Ten of Hearts—Dog

For once the interpretation of the card generally agrees with other systems. The Ten of Hearts is identified with a faithful dog. Dogs also appear in the eighteenth Tarot trump card, which is the Moon. The card indicates a lasting and loyal friendship. When it is found close to the significator, it denotes a relationship that should be nurtured, but when it is distant it can reveal deceit, illusion, and false friends (much as in the Tarot Moon card).

19   Six of Spades—Tower (Castle)

One never quite knows where one is with the Six of Spades in this system. The card is symbolized as a high tower or castle. Its proximity to the significator usually means protection and the likelihood of living to a ripe old age; however, if surrounded by bad cards, there is a kind of siege going on. Although the questioner is safe enough, nothing is actually being done to address his pressing problems. In this scenario, the tower can show sickness and debility.

20   Eight of Spades—Garden

In total contrast to other interpretations, this system makes this a happy card identifying the Eight of Spades with a Garden. It signifies parties, celebrations, and happy meetings. If it is close to the significator, it can refer to the formation of a lasting friendship;

but if it is distant, then casual acquaintances should not be fully trusted.

21 Eight of Clubs—Mountain

If this card is close to the significator, then it tells of a ruthless, powerful, and remorseless enemy. If it is distant, then loyal allies will help if peril threatens.

22 Queen of Diamonds—Roads

The card depicts an open road revealing the simplest and most obvious path out of trouble. However if the card is near the King of Clubs, then this escape route is obscured. It is up to the questioner to find it.

23 Seven of Clubs—Mouse (Mice)

The Seven of Clubs is considered an ominous symbol, as the mouse or mice symbolize robbery, deceit, and danger. The mouse nibbles away at the questioner's confidence and his possessions, so it is important to be extra vigilant when this card appears. If close to the significator, his possessions may be recovered, but if far away he may never see them again.

24 Jack of Hearts—Heart

According the Lenormand system, this card is all about true romance, long-lasting love, and joyful emotional contentment. She symbolized it simply as a heart.

25 Ace of Clubs—Ring

The Ace of Clubs is associated with a wedding or engagement ring in this system. If this appears to the right of the significator, it bodes well for his love life; but when to the left, it brings disappointment.

26 Ten of Diamonds—Book

This card suggests deep, dark secrets, so as the old saying goes, "Never judge a book by its cover"! The farther the book is away from the significator the better. However, if it is surrounded by positive cards, then keeping a secret will work in the questioner's favor.

27 Seven of Spades—Letter

This is a fairly neutral card. Obviously this means news from afar, but whether this is likely to be good or bad depends on the positive or negative nature of the cards surrounding it.

28 Ace of Hearts—Gentleman (Man)

This card is the significator for a male, so if the reading is for a man it has no real meaning. If a woman is the questioner, it might indicate that an important man is about to enter her life, but the rest of the reading will show the true picture—if indeed the card actually happens to be significant.

29 Ace of Spades—The Lady (Woman)

This card is the significator for a female. If the reading is for a woman, it has no real meaning, but if the questioner is male, it might indicate an important or influential woman coming into his life. The rest of the reading will throw light on the matter—if indeed there is one to consider.

30 King of Spades—Lily

The lily ensures a life that is both happy and virtuous, but its position in relation to the significator has a major influence on the card's interpretation. If the lily is found above the significator, then virtue will be rewarded by good fortune, but if it is found below, it is ominous and it would bring grief, uncertainty, and domestic upheavals.

31 Ace of Diamonds—Sun

This card has a happy meaning in the Lenormand system, foretelling good luck and joyous times. The closer it is to the significator, the better.

32 Eight of Hearts—Moon

If adjacent to the significator, this card is a good omen signifying honor, appreciation, and the respect of those around the enquirer. If far away then the meaning is the opposite with frustration and even grief as subsidiary interpretations.

33 Eight of Diamonds—Key

If this card is placed close to the significator, it is a positive indication as it brings success well beyond the questioner's expectations. A new doorway to accomplishment and satisfaction beckons. If the key is distant, there are problems to be solved and the questioner may lack the courage needed to reach his goals.

34 King of Diamonds—Fish

Stories about Mlle. Lenormand suggest that she did not like the King of Diamonds, and that she regarded its appearance as the mark of an opportunist and traitor. However, she also considered that it could foretell fortune, were the questioner willing to seize an opportunity. If the fish is far from the significator, then new ventures will be more difficult than anticipated.

35 Nine of Spades—Anchor

The classical symbol of hope is found near the end of Lenormand's sequence, and it indicates emotional and financial security. When close to the significator, this card is favorable, both in professional matters and affairs of the heart. When it is distant, it signifies a change of mind and direction.

36 Six of Clubs—Cross

The Six of Clubs is symbolized as a cross, and it is usually illustrated as a conventional crucifix. This is the last card in the Lenormand system, and unfortunately it is considered a bad omen and "a cross to bear." When it appears in close proximity to the significator then at least the ills it foretells will be of short duration.

20

Some Lenormand Spreads

As usual in all forms of card reading it is wise to do this when both the reader and the questioner are in a calm, receptive state of mind. First the reader and then the questioner should shuffle the deck thoroughly. The cards should then be handed back to the reader, who will lay them out in a meaningful pattern.

Laying Out the Cards

The simplest way of reading cards in the Lenormand style is simply to concentrate on your question and to draw out a single card. Just as in other methods of card reading, this card will give you the broad situation that is current in your questioner's life. You can do this for yourself on a daily basis in order to provide a general outlook for that day. (Rune readers tend to do much the same thing when they pick one rune from their bag each morning.)

To illustrate this for you, I have just shuffled the deck and drawn card 34, the Fish (King of Diamonds). This indicates that although I should be on the lookout for a self-seeking rogue, there is an opportunity in the offing that I would be wise to seize immediately. Well, I guess that I will have to wait and see what the day brings…

The Annual Spread

This is another very simple method of reading that employs twelve cards, each standing for a calendar month, starting with the month that you happen to be in. So if you are reading on August 12, then

August will be represented by the first card. No significator is required for this spread.

However, if either cards 28 (Ace of Hearts) or 29 (Ace of Spades) turn up as part of the reading, this is a signal that the questioner should follow his own desires and think of his own interests during that month.

If the significator for the opposite sex turns up, then that month could signal meeting the man or woman of his dreams.

The cards are laid out in a square of four by three. Beginning at the top left-hand corner, read the cards of each line in sequence to see what the general influences will be during each month.

1	2	3
4	5	6
7	8	9
10	11	12

Example:
The cards dealt on September 1 for a young woman who was contemplating a committed relationship but who was unsure of her intended partner's feelings, were as follows:

September: 26 Book (Ten of Diamonds). All is not as it seems, so be cautious when dealing with appearances.

October: 23 Mice (Seven of Clubs). Be cautious with both your possessions and your confidences.

November: 18 Dog (Ten of Hearts). A good and faithful friend will exert a positive influence.

December: 4 House (King of Hearts). A happy domestic environment is forecast for this month as well as a generally successful life.

January: 12 Birds (Seven of Diamonds). You may have to put up with a situation that is less than perfect but the difficulties that are experienced now will be short lived.

February: 13 Child (Jack of Spades). This is the time to open your heart, put old hurt aside, and forgive and forget. A sense of wonder returns.

March: 16 Stars (Six of Hearts). A very hopeful symbol, so be optimistic.

April: 17 Stork (Queen of Hearts). Travel is likely this month. If someone departs from you it will be a blessing in disguise.

May: 2 Clover (Six of Diamonds). This looks like a lucky season. The clover means good fortune in all that you do.

June: 31 Sun (Ace of Diamonds). Another happy symbol, because the sun promises good fortune.

July: 34 Fish (King of Diamonds). The fish show a golden opportunity now.

August: 22 Roads (Queen of Diamonds). The road that you should travel will become obvious in August. Do not hesitate.

Initially the cards warn the questioner not to be taken in by appearances. This trend continues in October, but by November there is an upswing in fortunes with the appearance of a faithful friend. After that her affairs improve month by month.

The Near and Far Spread

This is a twelve-card spread that surrounds the significator. The reader picks the significator out of the deck and puts it down, then lays the remaining cards around it. The significator for a man is the Ace of Hearts and for a lady it will be the Ace of Spades.

The cards are laid out with the significator face up, and the remaining cards face down in a cross pattern. There will be three cards above, three below, and three on either side of the significator. The reader starts by turning over two cards that are placed on each side of the significator, the two that are above, and the two that are below. He should read these eight cards first as they stand for the most important prevailing influences.

The correct sequence of the innermost cards is shown alphabetically in the following diagram.

A

B

G   **C**   **(Sig)**   **D**   **H**

E

F

The first eight cards are now read in sequence:

A, B, C, D, E, F, G, and H.

As in most readings by the Lenormand method, the reader should take note of obvious patterns developing between individual cards because these may provide new insights into the enquirer's situation. Let us look at an example that starts by examining the first eight cards that surround the significator.

Example:

This reading was done for a man in his mid-thirties who has suffered from both health and financial problems. Naturally, the significator is card 28, the Man (Ace of Hearts).

The eight closest cards were:

Position A	36 Cross (Six of Clubs)
Position B	6 Clouds (King of Diamonds)
Position C	8 Coffin (Nine of Diamonds)
Position D	14 Fox (Nine of Clubs)
Position E	23 Mice (Seven of Clubs)
Position F	11 Scourge (Jack of Clubs)
Position G	26 Book (Ten of Diamonds)
Position F	7 Snake (Queen of Clubs)

At first glance, the cards seem very grim indeed. The Cross in the first position looms over everything, showing a heavy burden, but this should be of short duration. This is emphasized by the Clouds sitting above the significator. This suggests that no matter how pressing or difficult life is to cope with at the moment, the troubles will eventually pass away. Ill health is shown by the Coffin in position C, and a general lack of support from supposed friends is indicated by the Fox in Position D.

All these factors have sapped the questioner's confidence and material resources (as shown by the Mice in Position E). Discord, marital breakup, or at least the loss of companionship are the results indicated by the Scourge.

The picture is not improved by the presence of the Snake, which governs new companions who only have their own interests at heart. Even so, the questioner should take note of the Clouds, which mean that even the hardest times will end; and also the Book, which indicates that not everything is known as yet.

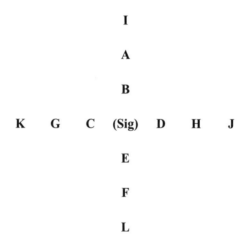

The further cards were:

Position I   17   Stork (Queen of Hearts)
Position J   31   Sun (Ace of Diamonds)

Position K   13   Child (Jack of Spades)
Position L   10   Scythe (Jack of Diamonds)

The further cards begin with the Stork showing feelings of abandonment, but the Sun shines in the next position foretelling a change of luck on the horizon. It may not be immediate but it is light at the end of a dark tunnel. The Child indicates a time when putting bitterness aside and learning to forgive will be very important. Finally, the Scythe paired with the positive Sun and Child mean that all difficulties will eventually be overcome and the bad times will move away, once and for all.

The Pyramid Spread

The Pyramid Spread is a little more complex, because ten cards are arranged around the significator in the form of a pyramid or triangle. Five cards form a line at the bottom, three (including the significator in the center) form the next line above, two are laid in the line above that, and finally a single card at the top represents the outcome.

```
                    10

           8                9

      6           Sig            7


1      2           3           4      5
```

The first thing to note is the number of beneficial or challenging cards in the reading, for this will set the tone for the whole prediction.

The lower five cards tell of the past and of events that have led to the present circumstances.

The cards in immediate proximity to the significator are the most important, as they are closest to the questioner's consciousness.

The two cards in the row above the significator represent the choices the questioner has to make.

The single card at the summit represents the outcome if the questioner does nothing other than follow the line of least resistance.

Example:

This reading was done for a woman in her early thirties after she had suffered a relationship breakdown and a business setback. In this case, the significator is card 29, the Lady (Ace of Spades). The cards dealt were as follows:

Lowest line from left to right, denoting the Past:

34 Fish	(King of Diamonds)
6 Clouds	(King of Clubs)
14 Fox	(Nine of Clubs)
12 Birds	(Seven of Diamonds)
9 Flowers	(Queen of Spades)

The appearance of the Fish suggests that a new venture in the past was more difficult than anticipated. Perhaps a golden opportunity was obscured by the Clouds along with the malice and deceit of the Fox.

The Birds suggest a sudden departure from a once-promising situation, while the next card, Flowers, urges one to leave the past behind and look to the future with confidence.

The cards indicating the present from left to right:

35 Anchor	(Nine of Spades)
The significator	(Ace of Spades)
22 Roads	(Queen of Diamonds)

The confident outlook is emphasized by the Anchor next to the significator on the next line. The Road the questioner must take is now obvious and it will lead her out of trouble.

The two cards showing what choices are to be made:

    1 Cavalier   (Nine of Hearts)
    13 Child   (Jack of Spades)

The Cavalier suggests lots of new and exciting things coming into the questioner's life. Roads in the pervious line implied that she would soon move on and now the Cavalier shows travel. So one choice she could make is to physically move, in addition to distancing herself from the past in an emotional sense. On the other hand, the Child suggests forgiveness, kindness, and letting bygones be bygones.

The outcome card:

    24 Heart   (Jack of Hearts)

The final card does not indicate which choice she will make, but it does show that whatever the questioner decides, true love and a lasting happy relationship lies in her future.

The most famous of all Mlle. Marie Lenormand's spreads is called the Master Method, in which all 36 cards are used. This spread is said to answer all possible questions, but it is so complex and it has so many stages of interpretation that I have broken it down into the two chapters that follow this one.

21

The Master Method

The Master Method is also called the "Square of Thirty-Six," and is said to be the system by which Mlle. Lenormand made some of her most famous predictions. It is therefore ironic that the first stage of this complex divination cannot be accomplished with some of the specialized types of cards that bear the illustrious lady's name. This is because the initial interpretation of the cards is based on the individual suits: Clubs, Diamonds, Hearts, and Spades. It would be difficult to use any deck that does not use these suits.

As usual with readings of the Lenormand type, the 36 cards are used both in their sense as a playing pack and in terms of their unique symbolism (see the chapter on the Lenormand System).

In the Master Method, all 36 cards are used in a six-by-six grid pattern. Each position in this pattern has an individual meaning of its own, relating to 36 different interests, issues, or sectors of life.

The first requirement of the Master Method is a large table. (You can also lay the cards out on the floor in order to accommodate then all.) The second requirement is a notebook to record the card positions, because it is unlikely that anyone would plough through every aspect of the reading at one sitting.

Another interesting variation found in this system is that the cards are not only read using the symbolic meanings of Mlle. Lenormand, but also with the interpretations given for the 32-card "Romany" deck (see the chapter on the Romany Way). So it will not only be necessary to mark your cards with the Lenormand number and symbol, but also to take into account the upright and reversed positions of the cards.

The deck is shuffled and cut in the usual way, and the reader then deals the cards face up according to the grid pattern from Position 1 to Position 36.

It would be a good idea to keep a notebook handy to jot down the cards in their relevant positions both by suit and card number.

Position 1	Position 2	Position 3	Position 4	Position 5	Position 6
Purpose	Accomplishment	Recognition	Expectation	Speculation	Wishes & desires
Position 7	**Position 8**	**Position 9**	**Position 10**	**Position 11**	**Position 12**
Wrongs & Injustices	Ingratitude	Contacts	Losses & Reversals	Problems	Possessions
Position 13	**Position 14**	**Position 15**	**Position 16**	**Position 17**	**Position 18**
Joy	Love & Affection	Welfare	Matrimony	Worries	Harmony
Position 19	**Position 20**	**Position 21**	**Position 22**	**Position 23**	**Position 24**
Windfalls	Dishonesty	Opposition	Presents	Friendships	Advancement
Position 25	**Position 26**	**Position 27**	**Position 28**	**Position 29**	**Position 30**
Cooperation	Undertakings	Circumstances	Sorrow	Appreciation	Scandal
Position 31	**Position 32**	**Position 33**	**Position 34**	**Position 35**	**Position 36**
Future Prospects	Affluence	Neglect	Awards	Influence & Power	Health

Remember that this system can be used in both the Romany and Lenormand manner, and you may even find that you can use both methods with a little practice.

The initial reading is of the suits only. However, certain cards have their own special meaning when found in a particular position.

These meanings will be dealt with under the appropriate heading at the end of this chapter.

Position 1—Present Purpose

This position refers to whatever is in the mind of the questioner. It may indicate an immediate project with a desired aim.

Clubs: A Club card in this position indicates that the help of friends will be necessary for the successful completion of a project.

Diamonds: Obstacles in business and financial affairs.

Spades: Worrying problems. Immediate action is needed to avoid failure.

Hearts: Proceed with your plans. You cannot fail with this symbol of success.

Position 2—Accomplishment

This position refers to what may be accomplished and what the questioner can expect to gain from the present purpose.

Clubs: Friendships and alliances will be strengthened, and they will overcome all difficulties.

Diamonds: Success, but petty spite arising from envy mars your satisfaction.

Spades: Little satisfaction because of overt opposition. Unfair tactics and deceit.

Hearts: A satisfying conclusion exceeding all your expectations.

Position 3—Recognition

The card here indicates the prestige that you will gain through your efforts and achievements.

Clubs: You will gain recognition through the influence of friends.

Diamonds: You will not gain as much recognition as you believe is due you. However, this minor success will lead on to greater things.

Spades: You reputation may suffer. You may be blamed for something that is not your fault. Envious rivals may block your efforts.

Hearts: Fame, an excellent reputation with congratulations from all
          sides.

Position 4—Expectation

This position is self-explanatory. It deals with what you expect to
happen, not necessarily what will actually occur.

Clubs: Be persistent now. Old friends may not be able to help you,
          but new people coming into your life will be more in tune
          with your aims.

Diamonds: Think big. Small ideas are not for you. Be ambitious
          and reach for the sky.

Spades: Unrealistic aims. Moderate your ambitions, at least for
          now. Only minor matters may be accomplished
          successfully.

Hearts: It is very lucky to find a Heart here. You will achieve
          something wonderful.

Position 5—Speculation

This position deals with risk, especially financial risk, and this may
constitute anything from placing a bet on the horses to speculating
on the stock exchange. Is luck on your side? Are you likely to be a
winner or a loser?

Clubs: Follow sound advice from a reliable person and you cannot
          go wrong.

Diamonds: You will suffer some losses but equally benefit from
          unexpected gains. If you are owed money then chase it now,
          otherwise you may never see it again.

Spades: Don't gamble! You cannot win at the moment, so attempt to
          cut your losses. You are at risk from the dishonesty of
          others.

Hearts: Any contemplated risk is likely to succeed. This is a signal
          to take a chance.

Position 6—Wishes and Desires

Obviously, this is what you hope to happen.

Clubs: Partial achievement of your desires, mainly through the influence of those who are well disposed toward you. If you really cannot get what you want, change your attitude and want what you get, as you will be happier that way.

Diamonds: You will have to push hard for what you desire. Friends will help if they are urged to, but you may still have to put up with second best. Don't give in to envy.

Spades: Spades are usually negative cards, and this one is no exception. Your chances are zero.

Hearts: Your desires will be fulfilled sooner than you expect.

Position 7—Wrongs and Injustices

This position is concerned with grievances that the questioner may have or injustices that have been done to him.

Clubs: Misunderstandings will be corrected by those who respect you. If you use friends as intermediaries, the situation will be rectified sooner.

Diamonds: Your reputation will not suffer, and those who have wronged you will make amends if you are magnanimous to them.

Spades: Turn your back on this and walk away! Any attempt to put things right will only make them worse.

Hearts: Any injustice will be rectified quickly, accusations will be proved false, and the whole unpleasant experience can now be turned to your advantage.

Position 8—Ingratitude

This position highlights the ingratitude of people and the products of their envious actions.

Clubs: Expressions of thanks may be a long time coming but come they eventually will.

Diamonds: There is a hidden motive at work. Be subtle and make some enquiries as to what actually is behind this spite.

Spades: It is your own fault. You have been too generous to unworthy people. Learn from experience and be more selective in your choice of friends.

Hearts: Be confident because you are better than those who envy you and they know it. Admiration will be expressed in the right quarters.

Position 9—Contacts

Dealings with work colleagues, business partners and clients can be seen in this position.

Clubs: All your dealings must be open and above-board, so there is no possibility of misunderstandings damaging your working relationships.

Diamonds: Don't be too ready to take sides in a dispute. If you do, you could end up being blamed for everything. Be tactful and keep your head down.

Spades: A worrying outlook where there are rivals for your position and a general lack of trust. Take what you can now and remove yourself from this poisonous situation quickly.

Hearts: Fulfilling relationships with colleagues. You can profit in financial affairs and also create lasting friendships.

Position 10—Losses and Reverses

Here the cards show where life's inevitable setbacks are likely to occur.

Clubs: A good friend leaves your company. This person will be missed.

Diamonds: Money problems are likely. Make sure that you have some savings.

Spades: This card is very dangerous when in this position. Your vital interests are at stake. Be careful and do not trust too readily.

Hearts: The loss of a person who has been a great support. You may have depended on this person too much, so this could be seen as a chance to stand on your own feet.

Position 11—Problems

This position deals with problems of a personal nature, although it may also stray into business matters.

Clubs: Disputes among friends could lead to a breakup of a group unless misunderstandings are resolved.

Diamonds: Quarrels over money, duty, or expectations will prove a serious headache.

Spades: Envy and resentment are at the root of all disputes.

Hearts: Your relatives will be troublesome, and family disputes could escalate into full-scale war unless this is dealt with quickly and firmly.

Position 12—Possessions

The card here deals with all your assets, from material possessions to your investments and security.

Clubs: Hard work and the healthy respect of your colleagues will ensure your prosperity.

Diamonds: Don't waste time or you will lose opportunities. There may be a dispute over property.

Spades: You are losing out due to a lack of vision. Fix on a new venture; the one you are pursuing now will not lead you to prosperity.

Hearts: A steady and continuing increase in affluence. There may be the possibility of an inheritance.

Position 13—Joy

This position analyzes your happiness quota.

Clubs: Pride in your work and in what you know that you can achieve will bring you lasting happiness. Friendships also bring joy into your life.

Diamonds: Material things will only bring you worry. Stop being so anxious and you will learn what true happiness really is.

Spades: Help others and you will help yourself. Your generosity and loyalty will be rewarded by people in lofty positions. However, if you are selfish you will not achieve happiness.

Hearts: Inspired thoughts and the finer things in life will bring you joy.

Position 14—Love and Affection

This is one of the most important positions in the entire reading. The card here could influence the whole tone of the interpretation.

Clubs: Constancy, fidelity, and dependability are the main features of the relationship.

Diamonds: A clash of personalities or interests will create resentment within a relationship. You may have a rival in love.

Spades: A bad omen for an existing relationship. Affections are fickle and may change on a whim. However there will be more luck in a new emotional link.

Hearts: Mutual understanding and also a meeting of minds, because a happy heart is the happy forecast of this card.

Position 15—Welfare

Prosperity and the way you look at your progress in life are shown in this position. It also shows the prevailing trend of life as a whole rather than the immediate here and now.

Clubs: Hard work may be wearing you out but keep at it! Do not lose sight of your ultimate goal and you will win through.

Diamonds: Your progress is hampered by the envy of those who are less talented than you. Keep your wits about you.

Spades: Someone or several envious people are maliciously placing obstacles in your path. You need to act against this willful antagonism.

Hearts: You will gain what you deserve, but since Hearts are considered a good omen, this should be to your benefit. Think big, because luck is with you.

Position 16—Matrimony

Although this position is traditionally associated with marriage, any long-term emotional commitment is represented here.

Clubs: A friendship develops into romantic love, which in turn becomes deep emotional commitment. You may meet through mutual friends. There will be a practical outlook within the marriage.

Diamonds: A good relationship is indicated, yet it is interrupted by jealous outbursts. Try to control these suspicions, otherwise the partnership will not succeed.

Spades: Unfaithfulness, jealousy, suspicion, and lies. If the 7, 8, or 9 are found here, the placement suggests divorce!

Hearts: A good and happy partnership with shared interests and a great mutual understanding. If the Ace of Hearts (the significator for a male) is found here, the outlook for future happiness is secure.

Position 17—Worries

This position represents underlying anxieties that may be unspoken. Although to others they may seem trivial they are actually very disturbing to the person who is afflicted by them.

Clubs: A conflict within a group of friends could have serious consequences. Kiss and make up or at worst, allow reconciliation to occur naturally. If it does not, then do your best to paper over the cracks and restore an amicable relationship.

Diamonds: Hasty words and angry exchanges are at the core of anxieties. Misunderstandings occur, but remember that you should not be too ready to take offense when none is intended.

Spades: Vicious criticism is the main cause of fear. You can do nothing but allow events to take their course and behave with dignity. Do not put yourself in a vulnerable position.

Hearts: You will worry about love, relatives, and friends (probably in that order). These anxieties are inevitable but they will soon pass.

Position 18—Harmony

This position shows how happiness and harmony in life can be achieved. In practice, this position talks about how we get along with others. All the cards here are interpreted in a positive light and should be regarded as advisory.

Clubs: Be good to people on the way up! Remember your true friends and do not be taken in by those of the fair-weather variety.

Diamonds: Loyalty must be your watchword. Form close alliances and side with your friends, even when you do not fully agree with their positions.

Spades: Cultivate new friendships. Many of those who you know right now are unsuitable and will drag you down to their level.

Hearts: Don't allow romance to turn your head away from those who have proved themselves by their loyalty and worth.

Position 19—Windfalls

In the old days this position was interpreted exclusively in terms of inheritance. Today we have other possible means of gaining unearned income – unlikely though it may be!

Clubs: A gain, possibly through the kindness of a friend or relative. It is also possible that one such windfall may be closely followed by another.

Diamonds: There may be a dispute over an inheritance or a win. This could go on for a long time. The stronger your rights the longer it will take for the issue to be resolved. You may not receive all that is due to you.

Spades: Beware of fraud. Check your affairs thoroughly and leave nothing to chance, otherwise you might never learn the truth.

Hearts: A large gain or opportunity. This will be far beyond your expectations. It is a long-term forecast. The longer you wait the better it will be for you.

Position 20—*Dishonesty*

This position deals with deceit and fraud as well as with untrustworthy people who as yet may have not shown their true colors. If a picture card is found here, it doubles the danger as well as giving a clue as to the identity of the double dealer.

Clubs: If you suspect underhanded dealings then seek professional advice at once. Your true friends will help you.

Diamonds: Be cool and confident because any plot against you will collapse.

Spades: You are in serious danger of having your reputation and your opportunities ruined by malicious deception.

Hearts: Any plot against you will backfire on the perpetrator. Hold your head up high and do not feel sorry for him, as he has only himself to blame!

Position 21—*Opposition*

In this position, the opposition to you is overt. Everything from friendly competition to hostile conflict is dealt with here. Although other positions show the causes of this opposition, it is the outcome that is indicated in this position.

Clubs: Teamwork is the key to success. With allies you can overcome opposition and prevent opponents ganging up on you.

Diamonds: Your opponents are divided, so even if they seem to be in a stronger position than you are, do not lose heart. You may win due to the fact that your competitors are not up to the challenge.

Spades: You do not have much hope of winning this conflict.

Hearts: You will have a complete and utter triumph over all opponents.

Position 22—*Presents*

This position covers gifts and tokens of esteem that you may receive.

Clubs: Practical gifts from friends and relatives.

Diamonds: Unwanted, useless gifts could put you under an obligation to a person who wants you to owe him a favor.

Spades: There is no such thing as a free lunch! There is likely to be hidden complications. Beware of participating in some shady scheme.

Hearts: High honors and generous gifts that are beyond your expectations.

Position 23—Friendship and Affection

The title of this position is self-explanatory and deals with the dependability and trustworthiness of those whom you spend time with.

Clubs: Good, honest, sincere friends on whom you can rely.

Diamonds: An argumentative and irritable circle of friends who have to be humored.

Spades: Trust actions rather than words, and you will soon find out who is false and who is not.

Hearts: You are the object of respect and affection. You will never want for true companionship.

Position 24—Advancement

This position deals with worldly status and how you may improve it.

Clubs: Hard work wins respect. You will gain advancement through people who you impress with your diligence.

Diamonds: If you are determined enough, you can achieve anything. You will be criticized but that should not put you off your goals.

Spades: The further you go the more envy you will meet. Rivals will try to block your progress and their success in this will depend on how determined you are to prevent this from happening.

Hearts: Expect sudden promotion or a rapid rise in status. This could indicate fame.

Position 25—Cooperation

This position shows how much you can depend on the help and advice of others when the pressure is on.

Clubs: All you have to do is ask and help will be immediately given.

Diamonds: Be self-reliant because help will be patchy at best.

Spades: Rely on your own efforts, because those around you will be no help at all—even if they wish to be.

Hearts: Help and excellent advice will come from a totally unexpected source.

Position 26—Undertakings

This position deals with long-term projects rather than immediate jobs in hand.

Clubs: Check your facts and do not rely on luck. Your friends and associates will back you up but the effort has to be yours.

Diamonds: Seek success in a unique field. Avoid established competition and concentrate on one of your talents. Any disputes will be bitter and they could ruin your chances.

Spades: Do not stick your neck out to take a big risk. Wait and let events take their course.

Hearts: Be ambitious. Think big and do not allow yourself to be persuaded by the doubts of others.

Position 27—Circumstances

This position assesses the possible advantages or disadvantages of major changes in your life.

Clubs: Accept change only if responsible advice is offered from a genuine person.

Diamonds: Stick to the tried and true. The familiar is comforting but the new will bring many quarrels and frustrations.

Spades: Hold fast to your position in the face of great opposition.

Hearts: If your present circumstances are ideal, then you could not want for more. If not, then the opportunity to improve matters will occur soon.

Position 28—Sorrow

The sorrow referred to here is usually due to bereavement, an unfortunate circumstance that we must all come to terms with in our lives. This position should be interpreted with sensitivity and tact.

Clubs: The death or permanent departure of a friend.

Diamonds: A shock to the system due to the unexpected loss of a friend or relative.

Spades: For once, the Spade reading is more positive. A death or departure will actually solve a problem for the questioner.

Hearts: The questioner will learn much or receive much as the result of a death or departure.

Position 29—Appreciation

The more mature the questioner, the more important this position becomes. It deals with the rewards one can expect from long service or the fulfillment of talent. It may refer to feelings of appreciation that have already been shown.

Clubs: Good friends think very well of you. If you went away, you would be greatly missed.

Diamonds: Sudden recognition will surprise and please you. However, a sudden rise to prominence will inspire some envy in others.

Spades: Disappointment and limited recognition for your efforts.

Hearts: You are greatly appreciated and many have cause to be grateful to you. You will be amply rewarded by fate for your kindness and abilities.

Position 30—Scandal

This position is self-explanatory; this is where secrets are revealed and tittle-tattle is rife.

Clubs: A lower card here (6, 7, 8, or 9) shows that an embarrassing personal secret comes to light. If a higher card is present (Ace, King, Queen, or Jack) then the scandal concerns a friend, but it is no less embarrassing to the questioner because of a feeling of guilt by association.

Diamonds: Keep silent and do not react to a scandal inspired by malice and spite.

Spades: Even if you are in the right and accusations made against you are false, you will still have to go through an unpleasant time.

Hearts: The scandal will be a nine-day-wonder. Rise above it and it will soon blow over.

Position 31—Future Prospects

This position is purely predictive, rather than dealing with known factors. Luck obviously plays a major part here and it is expressed according to the following suits.

Clubs: A golden opportunity will come through friends and social interactions.

Diamonds: It does not matter who stands in your way or who is envious of you, because you will turn the tables and progress, despite them or even because of them.

Spades: A nervewracking time. You will have to surmount difficulties, but you will get through with the help and support of those who love you.

Hearts: A truly amazing streak of luck is on its way.

Position 32—Affluence

Here the cards take a look at the financial fortunes.

Clubs: A shrewd attitude, good working relations, and a lot of effort will improve your position.

Diamonds: You will always make money—although keeping it is your problem. Be more cautious and do not lend so much to others.

Spades: You will work hard but in many cases your tasks will seem thankless. Financial rewards will be a long time coming. Beware of fraudulent dealings.

Hearts: A Heart here means wealth whether by inheritance, a win, or just rewards through the normal route of work.

Position 33—Neglect

This position refers to "blind spots" in life, the neglect of friends, family, and opportunities that can work against the questioner's interests.

Clubs: Neglecting your friends will eventually cause them to neglect you. Take time to renew your links with those who are important to you.

Diamonds: Your own lack of care for your interests and possessions is an open attraction to those who would take advantage of your goodwill.

Spades: You probably have lost out through lack of attention to your own interests. However whatever you have lost, you can still lose more. Halt the trend and take prompt action to secure your possessions and your emotional security.

Hearts: Indifference to the feelings of others will hurt your own interests. You may be working too hard and forgetting that there is more to life than ambition.

Position 34—Awards

This position deals with kindnesses and favors done for you, as well as more substantial benefits, which you may receive as a result of your own foresight. This could include such things as receiving a pension or a lump sum via an endowment or some other kind of long term saving scheme.

Clubs: This is a good omen showing that you are held in high regard. Others will do you favors.

Diamonds: Look out for self-seekers who would dearly like to lay their hands on your good fortune.

Spades: As usual, Spades are negative—so do not expect much either in the way of favors or financial benefits.

Hearts: A Heart here is excellent because it shows that everything will come your way sooner or later. All you have to do is be patient.

Position 35—Influence and Power

This position reveals how you should best use the power and influence that you have gained.

Clubs: You have leadership potential, and those who know you well look up to you.

Diamonds: Pursue your goals secretly and surprise the world when you achieve great things. As usual with Diamonds, envious people will snipe at you the further you go down the road to success.

Spades: You may be deluding yourself, so you may want to do something else with your life. If you follow your true instincts, the meaning of this Spade is very good.

Hearts: You will have more than enough influence in the world to satisfy anyone.

Position 36—Health

This is a delicate subject and should be treated with tact. It concerns possible accidents or illnesses and the questioner's physical reaction to them.

Clubs: A Club here is a warning of an impending illness.

Diamonds: A minor ailment, probably one that the questioner has suffered from before.

Spades: This is a bad one showing a major indisposition and a slow recovery.

Hearts: Any illness will be brief or extremely minor.

Cards to Look Out For

As can be seen, some positions in the Master Method are more important than others. When a reduced deck of cards is used, individual cards take on extra meanings depending on where they are placed.

The general rule here is that the higher the card (Ace, King, Queen, Jack, or Ten) the more impact it will have on the questioner's life.

The Aces in the Master Method

An Ace is always important, and it can indicate vital matters that depend on its suit. Remember that in this system, as in more general Lenormand readings, the Ace of Hearts represents the questioner if he is male, while the Ace of Spades becomes the significator if the questioner is female. One of these two Aces will become the central card of the next stage in the Master Method reading.

The Ace of Diamonds: generally represents a letter or news. If it is preceded by a Club, the news will concern business or money. If preceded by a Diamond, it concerns jealousy; if a Spade, the news the letter contains is bad, but if a Heart, then the news is about love or from a lover.

The Ace of Spades is a card of good omen in this system. Its position will give added information, as indeed will the suit of the card preceding it.

The Kings in the Master Method

The King of Clubs in position 14, 22, 23, 24, or 32 relates to the emotional self and to romantic fortunes. For a woman, the King of Clubs shows that she will meet and marry a good and generous man. For a man, the same King indicates a fair and honorable fight with a rival in love. If the King of Clubs falls on 18, 19, 20, 27, or 28, it shows a person who has power of attorney, possibly the guardian of a minor.

When the King of Diamonds is found in positions 14, 22, 23, 24, or 32, it means the precise opposite to the King of Clubs, indicating a mean and quarrelsome husband or lover. However, if this King is immediately preceded by any Club or Heart, then everything will turn out all right in the end.

The King of Spades on any of the positions numbered 14, 22, 23, 24, or 32 is even worse then the King of Diamonds.

The King of Hearts tends to be a good omen. In position 4, 13, 14, 15, 16, 18, 19, 23, 24, 29, 31, 32, or 34 it shows that despite all struggles, the questioner's wishes (whether male or female) will be completely fulfilled with regard to the meaning of that particular position. Some success is also shown if it falls on 1, 5, 6, 9, 12, 22, 26, 27, or 28. In the more negative positions 7, 8, 10, 11, 17, 20, 21, 30, 33, 35, and 36, the presence of the King of Hearts undoes much of the damage shown by Spades or Diamonds.

The Queens in the Master Method

For a male questioner, the Queen of Clubs in any of the emotional positions 14, 22, 23, 24, or 32 promises a wonderful relationship. However, for a woman, the meaning is more worrying, showing a rival in love who is attractive and charismatic.

The Queen of Diamonds in 14, 22, 23, 24, or 32 needs to be preceded by a Club or a Heart if a relationship is to stand the test of time.

The Queen of Spades is a good sign for a bachelor if found on one the above positions. It is bad for a married man though, showing infidelity and consequent domestic upheavals.

The Queen of Hearts emphasizes emotional happiness when found on any of the above positions.

The Jacks in the Master Method

The Jack of Clubs in positions 10, 17, or 36 indicates that the questioner will be asked for a loan, and this may put him in a difficult position.

The Jack of Diamonds in any of positions 14, 22, 23, 24, or 32 may indicate a foreign lover.

The Jack of Spades has no other special meaning other than its general interpretation.

The Jack of Hearts is even more of a charmer when found in positions 14, 22, 23, 24, or 32.

The Tens in the Master Method

The Ten of Clubs is especially lucky when found in position 3, 5, 15, 18, 19, 22, 25, 28, 31, or 32.

The Ten of Diamonds often means a voyage or a journey. If it falls between two Clubs, this will be to the good. If between two Diamonds, the result will be bad. Between two Spades, the journey will be long or the visit extended, and if between two Hearts, then it will be short.

The Ten of Spades has no special extra meaning.

The Ten of Hearts in position 10 is a lucky card signifying happiness and success. In position 14 it means a fulfilling love affair, and in position 16, a happy marriage. If it is found in the marriage position and a Jack or a Seven occupies 7, 15, 17, or 25 there will be several children. The Ten of Hearts is quite blissful when found in 18, 19, 31, or 32.

The Nines in the Master Method

The Nine of Clubs only derives an extra meaning from the card that it follows. If this Nine follows another Club then a gift of money can be expected. If it follows a Diamond the gift is probably small, perhaps more of a gesture than anything of real value. If preceded by a Spade there are strings attached, and if the Nine follows a Heart the gift is probably jewelry.

The Nine of Diamonds signifies news. If preceded by a Heart the news is good, if a Spade the news will be bad.

The Nine of Spades has no special extra significance.

The Nine of Hearts only has an extra meaning when it is found adjacent to the Seven of Clubs. In this case a promise made to the questioner will shortly be fulfilled.

The Eights in the Master Method

The Eight of Clubs has no special meaning in this method.

The Eight of Diamonds relates to short journeys. Its special significance is taken from the preceding card.

The Eight of Spades has no extra meaning.

The Eight of Hearts is a very good omen when found in positions 5, 9, 15, 18, 19, 22, or 31.

The Sevens in the Master Method

The Seven of Clubs is good for romantic prospects in positions 14, 22, 23, 24, or 32. It is very good indeed when found close to the Nine of Hearts.

The Seven of Diamonds may show a foreign girl when found in any of the above positions.

The Seven of Spades has no extra significance.

The Seven of Hearts signifies marriage if found in one of the above positions.

The Sixes in the Master Method

In the classic Romany style readings, the Sixes are discarded, but in the Master Method they do develop some interpretations for use with this system.

The Six of Clubs means a trusted friend. Its position will give added information, as will the suit of the card preceding it.

The Six of Diamonds has practically the same meaning as the Six of Clubs.

The Six of Spades indicates a woman who is of importance to the questioner. Its position will give added information as will the suit of the card preceding it.

The Six of Hearts represents a man who is of importance to the enquirer. Its position will give added information as will the suit of the card preceding it.

After sorting your way through the suits and special card meanings of all 36 positions you might be forgiven if you end up exhausted and fairly confused. The best thing to do is note down each card in its appropriate position, because some of them will be very important for the next phase of this complex reading.

22

The Master Method – Interpretation

This reading requires a certain amount of fiddling around before you can select the nine cards that can be read. It is best not to view this as a nuisance, but to see it as a way of getting away from the normal issues of daily life and of sliding into a slightly trancelike state of mind that will allow your intuition to flow into the reading.

All 36 cards must be laid out in six lines, each containing six cards. The reading will only work when the significator is surrounded by other cards, so it cannot work if the significator turns up on any of the four outside layers

Remember that the significator for a man is the Ace of Hearts, while the significator for a woman is the Ace of Spades.

The following illustration will work. It demonstrates a layout where the significator lies in the middle of the spread in the number 15 position. In this case, the reader can proceed, because the numbers that are highlighted (8, 9, 10, 14, 16, 20, 21, and 22) all become part of the nine-card reading. The remaining numbers that are not highlighted and that are not adjacent to the significator are ignored.

In the case of this enquirer, card 15, which is Welfare, signifies that his welfare and his life in general is the central issue. However, there are issues surrounding the ingratitude of others (8), his contacts (9), losses and reverses (10), his affections (14), and marital happiness (16). Worryingly, there are also questions about dishonesty (20) and the opposition of rivals (21). However, presents (22) are also shown which may help him in his difficulties. Let us

1	2	3	4	5	6
7	8	9	10	11	12
13	14	Sig	16	17	18
19	20	21	22	23	24
25	26	27	28	29	30
31	32	33	34	35	36

hope that the questioner does not have a Spade or a Diamond in that position, or his hopes may be blighted.

If your first spread places the significator at the edge of the 36-card square, the original method offered a number of convoluted ways of making up a nine-card square. This involved such things as taking the last three cards in the top row to form the top line, extracting the nearest cards to the one in question for the middle row, and then taking the last three cards in the row that precedes or follows the significator card. Confused? Well, so am I! The original instructions were more like those for a game of chess than anything else.

Frankly, your best bet here is to start all over again, and if it still does not work, try it once more. If the won't work after three goes, then either abandon the reading and do something different, or leave it for another day. It may be that the questioner shouldn't have a reading at this particular moment in time, perhaps because he needs to make decisions or take action himself before stopping to see what fate has in store for him.

Making Sense of the Nine-Card Spread
To give some order and a sense of narrative to the nine-card spread, start with the lowest horizontal row of cards and take these to represent the past. The cards on the same horizontal row as the

significator show the present influences while the three cards above show the future. The three vertical cards to the left of the significator will tend to work against the questioner, even if their positions appear to be positive. Those on the right will tend to work for him, even if they seem negative—in which case they will represent blessings in disguise. The card immediately below the significator reveals the questioner's inner motivations while the one above shows his hopes or fears.

This is the stage of the reading where one has to make a choice. Either the individual card interpretations are taken from the Romany method or from the unique Lenormand system. It is even possible to use both systems concurrently, but you may need the brain of an Einstein to cope with this. I have given both types of reading in the example below, so I leave it to you to choose which you wish to use. Naturally, you could do a reading using the Romany method and then a second one using the Lenormand method.

Example:

Let us assume that one is reading for a man and the Ace of Hearts (the significator) appears in position 28. The relevant cards for the nine-card spread are as shown in the following diagram.

The background to the reading

The first thing to notice is that the significator occurs at position 28, which relates to Sorrow. Therefore, the questioner is carrying a burden that lies heavy on his heart. The past (represented by the cards below the significator) seem to be positive enough, although the King of Hearts is considered to be in negative in position 35, which relates to Influence and Power. On the other hand, the lower rank of cards is made up of two Hearts and a Diamond, so this is not a bad sign in itself. The Jack of Hearts at position 33 shows that the questioner has been indifferent to the feelings of others—also the possibility that the questioner has been working too hard or that he has been very distracted. This is likely to have provided an opportunity for false, self-seeking friends to worm their way into the

Position 21	Position 22	Position 23
Opposition 10 of Clubs (Bear – card 15)	Presents 6 of Diamonds (Clover –card 2)	Friendships 6 of Clubs (Cross – card 36)
Position 27	**Position 28**	**Position 29**
Circumstances Queen of Diamonds (Roads – card 22)	Sorrow Ace of Hearts (Man – card 28)	Appreciation 9 of Hearts (Cavalier – card 1)
Position 33	**Position 34**	**Position 35**
Neglect Jack of Hearts (Heart – card 24)	Awards Jack of Diamonds (Scythe – card 10)	Influence & Power King of Hearts (House – card 4)

questioner's confidence, as shown by the Jack of Diamonds in position 34 (Awards).

The Heart (24) and the Scythe (10) lead us to assume that the questioner has been too easy going and that this has caused the problem. We can see that the situation that has arisen from the past just cannot continue. However, the King of Hearts in position 35 undoes much of the damage done by these so-called friends—but even so, the realization must hurt the questioner deeply. This King becomes the House (4) in Lenormand's system, and this may literally refer to the questioner's home as well as his sense of personal security. The card advises caution when dealing with neighbors – or in this case, with friends.

The present

Moving on to the present influences, the significator is flanked by the Queen of Diamonds and the Nine of Hearts in positions 27 and 29—these are Circumstances and Appreciation respectively. A Diamond in position 27 would normally mean that the questioner should stick to what is familiar come what may. However, the card appears on the left of the significator, so it will work against the questioner's interests—this could indicate a change in circumstances is needed. In Lenormand's system this card is known as Roads (22) and so it reveals the simplest and most obvious route out of trouble.

The Nine of Hearts in position 29 is a very good sign. Any Heart here means that others respect and appreciate the questioner and the fact that many people have cause to be grateful to him. The Nine specifically reveals an antidote to the questioner's troubles and it assures him that these will soon be behind him. Celebrations are likely in the near future. According to Lenormand, the Cavalier (1) brings messages of good cheer and the possibility of travel.

The future

The three cards in the rank above the significator reveal the future. These are the Ten of Clubs in position 21 (Opposition), the Six of Diamonds in position 22 (Presents), and the Six of Clubs in position 23 (Friendship).

A Club card in position 21 would normally show that there are people upon whom the questioner can rely and that teamwork is the key to his success. However, the card occurs to the left of the significator, so it may hint that a little more self-reliance would be in order, bearing in mind the self-seeking nature of some of his colleagues. The Ten of Clubs is an indicator of luxury and prosperity that could come his way if he follows the card's advice. In Mlle. Lenormand's system this card is the Bear (number 15), so it reveals the envy of others and it urges the questioner not to be too trusting.

The presence of a Diamond in position 22 emphasizes gifts that may be useless or unwanted. The givers of these white elephants wish to put the questioner under an unwelcome obligation. Of course in the Romany method sixes have no meaning, but according to Lenormand the card becomes the lucky Clover (number 2) showing that good fortune will soon come along.

It is always lucky to have a Club in position 23 of Friendship and Affection. It reveals the influence of true, good, honest, and sincere friends to come. Although the sixes have no meaning in the Romany method, according to Mlle. Lenormand, this card is symbolized by the Cross (number 36). This shows that the obligations that the questioner owes are indeed heavy ones and that the problem cannot be solved overnight. He will have to carry the burden of the past with him for some time. Yet this and other cards show that he will have the help and advice of those who have his best interests at heart.

All the cards in the top rank indicate the influence of one or more good friends who will guide the questioner and help him to cope with his difficulties. Both the Six of Diamonds and the Six of Clubs have practically the same meaning—a trusted friend. The suit of the card that precedes them gives added information. In this case, the preceding card is the Ten of Clubs. Therefore if the questioner follows his new friend's advice, he will prosper.

It can be seen that the Master Method is an extremely complex system, which yields a wealth of information. It takes quite a lot of practice to gain a thorough understanding of the method, yet I feel sure that it would be worth the bother for anyone who is interested in reading the cards. After all, it is this method which gave Mlle. Lenormand some of her most important insights and which won her the reputation as one of the most accurate card readers of all time.

Editor's note: *Many years ago I became friendly with two card reading sisters who belonged to a Romany family. They used methods that were very similar to this, although they only used the Romany card interpretations. Their skill, along with a strong dose of intuition, made them among the best readers that I have come across – and I have met many in my time!*

23

Interpreting the Reading

Choosing the Significator

Most card spreads require a card that represents the questioner, and this card is called a significator. There are several ways of choosing an appropriate card for this purpose. The first harks back to the work of Etteilla and it is used for both the 52-card Poker deck and the 32-card Romany Deck. Here the card reader selects a card that most closely resembles the questioner's appearance, character, and coloring. For instance, the Queen of Diamonds may represent a forceful woman, while the Queen of Hearts would symbolize a fair, sensitive, artistic woman. Etteilla also said that the significator could be chosen by the questioner's profession or circumstances. Thus the King of Spades can denote a lawyer, while the Queen of Spades may suggest a widow or an independent woman.

Another point to bear in mind is that whatever King or Queen is chosen to be the significator, if the consort of that card appears in the reading, it will represent the questioner's spouse or partner. Thus the wife of a lawyer symbolized by the King of Spades will be depicted as the Queen of Spades, even though the lady is not a widow or independent. Jacks are usually youthful and they may be of either gender.

The astrological attributions provided by the Golden Dawn may also suggest a means for choosing a significator card, because each of the court cards is associated with a particular sign of the zodiac. The details about the traditional appearance, life-roles, and associated zodiac signs for each court card are given in sections dealing with the Kings, Queens, and Jacks.

Shuffling and Cutting

Before embarking upon the reading, it is essential that the reader be in a calm and receptive frame of mind. A few deep breaths and perhaps a little prayer might help achieve this passive yet aware state. The reader should initially shuffle the deck and then hand them to the questioner. If the reader is reading his own cards then he can now move to the cutting stage. After the questioner has shuffled the cards to his satisfaction, he should put them face down on the table and cut them into two piles. He should then choose one of the two piles to be used for the reading. This method will do for most ordinary purposes.

It is usual to start with a general spread that does not require a question. After this is finished, the reader should repeat the process from the beginning, this time asking the questioner to ponder on his question while he is shuffling and cutting. Remember that flippant questions will receive flippant answers. These will be of no use to the questioner and a waste of the reader's time, knowledge, and energy.

Before the Reading Starts

It is interesting to note that one can gauge the questioner's state of mind and character while he is shuffling and cutting the cards.

When the questioner hardly shuffles the cards at all, it reveals that he is extremely eager to get on with the reading. This may indicate impatience.

If any cards fall out while the client is shuffling, remember to take note of them, because they will prove to be important later.

If many cards fall out while the questioner is shuffling (whether or not the person is used to handling cards) he is likely to be indifferent, ambivalent, or reluctant to have a reading in the first place. The same applies if the questioner cuts the cards by taking very few cards from the topmost part of the deck. The same also applies if several cards fall from the cut portion of the deck while it is in the questioner's hand. All of the above reveals that the questioner does not really want to ask his question, or that he is afraid that the cards will reveal too much.

Those who are impressionable and introverted tend to cut the cards with their faces very close to the deck. This type of questioner must be treated with kid gloves because he will take your interpretations very literally—even if he tries to say that he is skeptical. Another type of questioner who concentrates deeply on the cutting, unconsciously moving his face to within inches of the deck, is likely to be deeply worried about something. These people try to cut the deck in the dead center if they can possibly manage it. This is because they are concerned to get the reading "right." People who are very worried need careful handling, and they can be demanding to read for because they want exact predictions, clear choices, and black-and-white alternatives.

People who are open minded but who cannot decide whether they believe in divination or not will tend to cut the cards into several piles.

Those who are confident that the cards will tell them what they expect usually sit back from the table with a smile on their faces and their arm extended while they are cutting the cards.

Some people do not look at the cards while shuffling and cutting them. They then hand them straight back to the reader or expect the reader to replace the cards into one deck. These people are rarely interested in having a reading at all and they only request one in the vague hope of proving the reader to be wrong.

Reading the Cards

Whatever spread you use, there are a couple of stages to go through before interpreting the individual cards. The first (and most obvious) thing to notice is the "color" of the reading. Playing cards are either red or black—Hearts and Diamonds being red and Spades and Clubs, black. A reading that is predominantly red is likely to be more positive than one that is mainly black.

Look out for any meaningful combination of cards, such as three Jacks, four Aces, three Twos, and so on.

The final stage, of course, is to read the cards in sequence following the rules within your chosen spread.

Spreads for the Poker Deck

The Single Card

This is simplest spread of all because it consists of a single card from which the reader draws and interpretation. It still requires a calm and passive state of mind, and it seems to work best when a specific question is asked. I have known some card readers to use this method like a horoscope in a daily newspaper to give them a general indication of the day ahead.

Example: I have just drawn the Seven of Spades, which urges me to keep my cool despite the provocations of a turbulent emotional atmosphere that happens to be around me at the moment.

The Three-Card Spread

This spread is a little more detailed. Again the cards are shuffled and cut, and three cards are laid in a row.

Read from left to right with A representing the past, B the present, and C the future. This spread is a good indicator of general

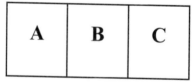

trends but it suffers due to the shortage of cards within it, so it cannot be too specific.

Example: The cards drawn are (A) Ace of Clubs, (B) Two of Diamonds and (B) Ten of Spades.

The Ace of Clubs suggests that the questioner has received good news in the recent past, and it also shows that he has enormous potential. Since it is the first card, it signifies that the questioner is a person of great talent and that this could take him a long way if he learns to channel his talents correctly.

The present is represented by the Two of Diamonds, which is another card of good news indicating a windfall or some other kind of material good fortune. It may also show that there are indirect benefits to the questioner because of another's luck. The card also reveals that fate or karma is working positively within the questioner's life.

The immediate future looks troublesome due to the Ten of Spades, which reveals that the questioner is about to reach the end of a long-drawn-out phase. He may be disillusioned and somewhat bitter because life has not given him what he thinks he deserves. On a brighter note, the card signals that now he has a blank slate and that he can begin something totally new.

The Magic Square

The Three-Card Spread can be extended into the Magic Square of nine cards. This can be used to add more detail to the sometimes, bland responses given by the previous spread.

The first step is to choose a court card to represent the questioner. This is removed from the deck and placed in the middle of the reading area to become the central card of the spread. After shuffling and cutting in the usual way, the rest of the cards are laid out in the following pattern:

Each position has an individual meaning:

A	B	C
D	E	F
G	H	I

Card A   The characteristics or the attitude of the questioner.

Card B   People surrounding the questioner.

Card C   Things that are unchanging and stable within the questioner's life.

Card D   Where the questioner will not compromise.

Card E   The Significator – the card that represents the questioner.

Card F   Opportunities that exist.

Card G   The questioner's beliefs.

Card H   The pessimistic outlook.

Card I   The optimistic outlook.

For an extended version of this classic spread, see The Master Method in this book.

The Date of Birth Spread

The basic three-card spread is very adaptable. In this variation, a method of card counting is used based on a person's date of birth to find three cards to answer a specific question. The full deck is shuffled and cut in the usual way while the questioner thinks of the issue at hand. The reader then deals the number of cards corresponding to the day of the month on which the questioner was born. Therefore, if he was born on the tenth, it is the tenth card that is chosen. Once this is done, the reader deals the number of cards corresponding to the month of birth—so if it were April, the fourth card is chosen, if December then it is the twelfth. A little basic numerology comes into play now to find the card corresponding to the birth year. Add together all the digits of the questioner's year of birth. Let us say it was 1981.

$1 + 9 + 8 + 1 = 19$. Now add $1 + 9 = 10$. Continue the process by adding $1 + 0 = 1$. Therefore the questioner's birth year corresponds to the very first card that is to be dealt.

If a questioner's birth date was August 9, 1975, the first card to be chosen is the ninth dealt. The cards are dealt again and the eighth is chosen, corresponding to August, which is the eighth month. Then the digits of the birth year are added $1 + 9 + 7 + 5 = 22. 2 + 2 = 4$. The cards are dealt again and the fourth card is chosen.

The Recitation Spread

After the preliminary shuffling and cutting, the reader should take the full deck. The Joker in the spread counts as a picture card. Deal each card in turn while reciting the following:

"Diamond, Club, Heart, Spade, Picture."

If the card turned is the same suit as the word that is spoken, then this card is put aside to form part of the reading. For instance, when the reader says "Diamond" and the Four of Diamonds turns up, then this card is part of the reading, but if that card were to appear when the reader says "Spade" it would not. The same applies for picture cards because even when one says "Club" and the Queen of Clubs appears it is discounted because it did not appear when the reader said, "Picture". In short the court cards are only allowed to become part of the reading when the word "Picture" is said, effectively making them into another suit.

Go through the entire deck in this fashion while reciting the formula of "Diamond, Club, Heart, Spade, Picture" in strict rotation. By the time you have reached the end of the deck you should have several cards placed in a row ready for interpretation.

Here is an example of the Recitation Spread in action. The following fifteen cards were the result:

3 Diamonds, 5 Hearts, K Spades, 4 Diamonds, 2 Spades, 5 Diamonds, 2 Clubs, A Spades, Q Diamonds, J Hearts, A Clubs, Q Clubs, 2 Hearts, 7 Diamonds, 6 Clubs.

Now the usual rules of card grouping apply. The predominant suit is Diamonds, suggesting practical or financial issues are the central issue of the reading. The main color of the reading is optimistic red, and there are two Aces, two Queens, three Twos, and two Fives. There are eight red cards and seven black cards. After these cards are interpreted according to their grouping the individual cards than then be read in sequence.

The Horseshoe Spread

Otherwise known as the Bohemian Spread, this is useful for a general reading or for answering specific questions. The full deck is shuffled and cut at usual; then it is spread out on the tabletop in the shape of a fan. The questioner then selects seven cards from anywhere in the fan and hands them to the reader, who then places them face down in the following pattern:

A						G
	B				F	
		C		E		
			D			

Card A: Past influences that have a bearing on the present.

Card B: The choices that the questioner now faces.

Card C: What the questioner desires or fears.

Card D: The challenges the questioner must face.

Card E: Help or hindrances.

Card F: Friends and foes.

Card G: The outcome.

The Celestial Circle Spread

This is traditionally used as a birthday or annual reading. No specific question is required because each card will reveal the prevailing influences throughout a month. Begin at the month one is in, even if it is the last day of that month). The thirteenth card is placed in the center, and it gives the general indication of fortune running through the full year.

The thirteenth card is interpreted by its suit alone, so if it is a Club the outlook for the coming year concerns the recognition of efforts and achievements, if a Diamond the main concern is material and financial, Spades indicate a troublesome time, while a Heart signifies a happy and emotionally fulfilling year ahead.

After shuffling and cutting in the usual way, the cards are laid out like a clock face and read like the hours on a clock, starting at 1 o'clock and ending at 12 o'clock.

This spread (like most of the others) can be used with any of the card reading systems within this book as well as with Tarot cards. A similar spread is utilized in the Lenormand system.

The Horoscope Variation Spread

This spread can also be adapted into a horoscope. The formation of the spread is the same as the Celestial Circle but the first card to be read is in the 9 o'clock position and the cards are read in a counter-clockwise direction from that point. This layout is familiar to every astrologer as the cards now lie in the positions of the astrological houses of the horoscope, each of which relates to a facet of life.

Card 1: The questioner's personality and self-expression.
Card 2: His values and possessions.
Card 3: Siblings, early education, local travel.
Card 4: Background, family life, and home.
Card 5: Romance, creativity, leisure activities, children.
Card 6: Work, health and habits.
Card 7: Long term relationships and rivalries.
Card 8: Sex, psychology, and anything that is shared with another.
Card 9: Beliefs, philosophy, and distant travels.
Card 10: Career, ambitions, and status.
Card 11: Friends, hopes, and wishes.
Card 12: Secrets and that which is confining.
Card 13: Overview and the influences of fate.

The Mystic Cross Spread

This is a thirteen-card spread that requires a previously selected significator to represent the questioner. The significator card may be chosen by the questioner's gender, coloring, profession, or star sign.

Twelve cards are dealt at random from the full deck after the usual shuffling and cutting. The significator is placed among these and the process of shuffling and cutting performed again with the thirteen cards. The thirteen cards are laid out in the following cross-shaped pattern.

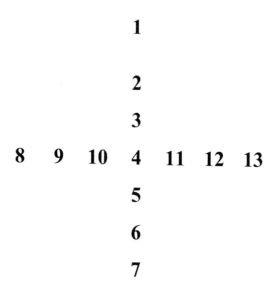

The vertical row refers the questioner's present circumstances and it is read from top to bottom. The horizontal row refers to outside influences that will affect the questioner's life. This row is read from left to right.

The first thing to look out for is the position of the significator. If it is found in the vertical row it means that the questioner is struggling with circumstances that are beyond his control. If it falls in the horizontal row it means that the questioner is in command.

The central card at the intersection of the two rows (in position 4) is the factor around which the whole situation revolves. It is the key to the spread and it can often provide the answer that the questioner seeks. If the significator is found in this position, then anything that the questioner intends to do is the right thing.

The Fan Spread

This spread requires the choice of a significator. This is not removed and the deck should be shuffled and cut in the usual way. The reader then deals thirteen cards. These are then checked to see if the significator is present, without changing the order of the cards. If the significator is not there, then the Seven of the same suit may be used as a substitute. If neither is present, then the reading is abandoned and the whole process begins again.

If either the significator or the Seven are there, then the cards are laid out in a fan from left to right with their edges slightly overlapping. The questioner then randomly selects five further cards from the deck, and these are laid out in a row below the fan of cards.

The cards in the fan are interpreted first. These reveal the immediate past and the current situation. The reader must now find the significator or its substitute, and count along toward the right until he reaches the fifth card. When this card has been interpreted, he counts along another five to find the next card. When all the cards (with the exception of the significator or its substitute) have been read in this fashion, the reader can move on to the future with the five cards below the fan.

The five "future" cards are read in pairs starting at both ends of the row. These two pairs reveal the options open to the questioner. This leaves card one remaining card, which signifies the outcome and the likely decision that will finally be reached.

This spread has certain similarities to both the ancient French and Italian Methods that can be found in the chapter on reading the Romany Deck.

24

Traditional Romantic Games and Readings

In addition to formal readings with the cards laid out in a pattern there are a number of traditional games, which were played with an eye to foreseeing the future. Unmarried girls usually played these games in a light-hearted manner as a welcome change from sewing and embroidery. As might be expected, most of the young ladies' questions involved marriage and romance—usually combined with a lot of giggling and teasing.

The Lottery of Love

This is very simple gambling game that any number of people can play. It requires a deck of cards, a large bag, and whatever change you have in your pocket. First place all the stakes in a pool, then shuffle the cards and place them in the bag. The players then form a circle and each draw three cards from the bag.

Should any player make a pair of any kind, she immediately wins back her stake and additionally has the promise of good luck in the near future.

If any player draws out a Four or an Eight, these are described as "Losses and Crosses" and she has to immediately double her stake and add it to the pool. This is not considered a fortunate omen.

If three Nines are drawn then single life is forecast. Three Fives forecast a bad and neglectful husband.

The best card to draw is the Jack of Hearts, who still sports little wings and wields a bow as Cupid. This card not only wins the game and clears the pool but also has the forecast of blissful love, and a long and happy marriage.

Another Love Lottery
This game requires an uneven number of young ladies. The cards are shuffled and placed into a bag. Each girl draws out one card in turn and shows it to the others.

The girl who draws the highest card will be the first to wed. The unfortunate girl who draws the lowest must be content to wait. If the Ace of Spades is chosen, then it is a single life for her! The Nine of Hearts has a sting though, because although this is the "wish card" and does deliver the person she desires, this lady will have cause to regret it because her longing will have serious and unpleasant consequences.

The players continue to pick cards out of the bag until they have read their fortunes to each player's satisfaction.

The Cupid and Venus Game
This game is a variant of whist. Any number of people can play. The cards are dealt equally between the players leaving ten cards face downward on the table. At this point gambling stakes are usually agreed upon, the dealer initially having to stake double the amount of the other players.

The most valuable card in this game is the Ace of Diamonds, and this should be the first card to be played.

The Queen of Hearts puts on her identity as Venus, the goddess of desire. The other Queens represent women, while all Kings represent men.

The Jack of Hearts is identified with Cupid, god of love.

The Jacks of Diamonds, Clubs and Spades represent sweethearts.

The Ace of Hearts means a new house.

The Ace of Clubs represents a conquest or seduction.

The Two of Diamonds denotes a wedding ring.

All Threes show surprises.

All Fours are static showing no change at all in present
    circumstances.

The Fives indicate lovers' meetings.

The Sevens indicate disappointment.

The Eights are indicative of laughter and fun.

The Nines show profound and far-reaching changes. The Nine of
    Spades is the worst card and condemns its possessor to a
    forfeit.

The game is played by throwing in and picking up cards to make up
tricks, and the more of these that the player has the better. In terms
of divination, the more tricks one has, the more luck one will have
throughout the coming year.

    If any player should hold both the Queen and Jack of Hearts,
then wedding bells are in the air, while any player holding the Ace
of Diamonds is assured of wealth.

Index

Aces, 26–31
  of Clubs, 28, 95, 129, 157
  combinations of, 104
  of Diamonds, 29, 97, 130, 157
  of Hearts, 31, 101–102, 130
  historical perspective, 16–17
  in Master Method, 157
  of Spades, 30, 99, 130, 157
  symbolism overview, 26–27
Annual Spread, 132–134
Cartomancy origin, 8–9
Casanova, 9–10
Celestial Circle Spread, 174–175
Clubs, 21
  Ace, 28, 95, 129, 157
  2 (Two), 33
  3 (Three), 38
  4 (Four), 43
  5 (Five), 48
  6 (Six), 53, 131, 160
  7 (Seven), 58, 97, 129, 160
  8 (Eight), 63, 97, 129, 159
  9 (Nine), 69, 96, 127, 159
  10 (Ten), 74, 96, 127, 158
  Jack, 79, 96, 127, 158
  King, 89, 95–96, 126, 157
  Master Method meanings, 142–156
  Queen, 84, 96, 126, 158

Romany Method meanings, 95–97
Combinations, of cards, 22–25
Cupid and Venus Game, 179–180
Curse of Scotland, 67–68
Cutting, 168
Date of Birth Spread, 172
Decans
  defined, 16
  elements, zodiac and, 16–18
Deck of cards, 1–20
  history. See History, of cards
  mystery of, 3–5
  overview, 1–2
  poker deck, 18–20
  preparing, caring for, 3
  Tarot and, 1–2, 8, 15–16
  time pattern, 4–5
"Deck of Cards" ballad, 6–7
Devil's picture book, 5–6
Diamonds, 21–22
  Ace, 29, 97, 130, 157
  2 (Two), 34
  3 (Three), 39
  4 (Four), 44
  5 (Five), 49
  6 (Six), 54, 125, 160
  7 (Seven), 59, 99, 127, 160
  8 (Eight), 64, 99, 130, 159
  9 (Nine), 70, 98, 126, 159

10 (Ten), 75, 98, 129, 159
Jack, 80, 98, 126–127, 158
King, 90, 97–98, 131, 157
Master Method meanings,
    142–156
Queen, 85, 98, 129, 158
Romany Method meanings,
    97–99
of Spades, 157
Eights, 62–66
of Clubs, 63, 97, 129, 159
combinations of, 106–107
of Diamonds, 64, 99, 130,
    159
of Hearts, 66, 103, 130, 159
in Master Method, 159
of Spades, 65, 101, 128, 159
symbolism overview, 62
Elements, 16, 17, 18
Etteilla, 10–11
Fan Spread, 177
Fives, 47–51
of Clubs, 48
of Diamonds, 49
of Hearts, 51
of Spades, 50
symbolism overview, 47
Fours, 42–46
of Clubs, 43
of Diamonds, 44
of Hearts, 46
of Spades, 45
symbolism overview, 42
French method, 113–118
Hearts
Ace, 31, 101–102, 130, 157
2 (Two), 36

3 (Three), 41
5 (Five), 51
6 (Six), 56, 127–128, 160
7 (Seven), 61, 103–104, 126,
    160
8 (Eight), 66, 103, 130, 159
9 (Nine), 72, 103, 125, 159
10 (Ten), 77, 102–103, 128,
    159
Jack, 82, 102, 129, 158
King, 92, 102, 125, 157–158
Master Method meanings,
    142–156
Queen, 87, 102, 128, 158
Romany Method meanings,
    101–104
History, of cards
cartomancy origin, 8–9
Casanova and, 9–10
"Deck of Cards" ballad, 6–7
devil's picture book and, 5–6
Etteilla and, 10–11
Golden Dawn and, 15–18
King Charles and, 5–6, 8
Marie Ann Adelaide de
    Lenormand and, 11–15
origin and, 7–8
Horoscope Variation Spread,
    175
Horseshoe Spread, 174
Interpreting readings
choosing significator,
    167–168
Master Method, 162–166
reading cards, 169–170
shuffling, cutting and, 168
Italian method, 118–123

Jacks, 78–82
  of Clubs, 79, 96, 127, 158
  combinations of, 105–106
  of Diamonds, 80, 98,
    126–127, 158
  of Hearts, 82, 102, 129, 158
  in Master Method, 158
  of Spades, 81, 100, 127, 158
  symbolism overview, 78
Jokers, 93
Kings, 88–92
  of Clubs, 89, 95–96, 126, 157
  combinations of, 104–105
  of Diamonds, 90, 97–98, 131,
    157
  of Hearts, 92, 102, 125,
    157–158
  in Master Method, 157–158
  of Spades, 91, 99–100, 130
  symbolism overview, 88
Lenormand, Marie Ann
  Adelaide de, 11–15
Lenormand spreads, 132–139
  Annual Spread, 132–134
  laying out cards, 132
  Near and Far Spread,
    134–137
  Pyramid Spread, 137–139
Lenormand system, 2–3, 14–15,
  124–131
  card meanings, 124, 125–131
Lottery of Love, 178–179
Magic Square, 171–172
Master Method, 140–160
  card priorities, 156
  interpretation, 161–166
  nine-card spread, 162–166

  overview, 140–142
  position meanings, 142–156
  summary chart, 141
Meanings, of cards. *See also*
  specific card names
  Lenormand system, 124,
    125–131
  poker deck, 18–20
Mystic Cross Spread, 175–176
Near and Far Spread, 134–137
Nine-card spread, 162–166
Nines, 67–72
  of Clubs, 69, 96, 127, 159
  combinations of, 106
  Curse of Scotland and, 67–68
  of Diamonds, 70, 98, 126,
    159
  of Hearts, 72, 103, 125, 159
  in Master Method, 159
  of Spades, 71, 100–101, 131,
    159
  symbolism overview, 67
Past, Present and Future Spread,
  110–113
Petit Lenormand system. *See*
  Lenormand system
Poker deck cards
  combinations, 22–25
  groupings, 21–25
  meanings, 18–20
  suits, 21–22
Poker deck spreads, 170–177
  Celestial Circle Spread,
    174–175
  Date of Birth Spread, 172
  Fan Spread, 177
  Horoscope Variation Spread,

175

Horseshoe Spread, 174

Magic Square, 171–172

Mystic Cross Spread,
175–176

Recitation Spread, 173

single card, 170

Three-Card Spread, 170–171

Preparation for readings,
168–169

Pyramid Spread, 137–139

Queens, 83–87

of Clubs, 84, 96, 126, 158

combinations of, 105

of Diamonds, 85, 98, 129,
158

of Hearts, 87, 102, 128, 158

in Master Method, 158

of Spades, 86, 100, 126, 158

symbolism overview, 83

Reading cards, 169–170

Recitation Spread, 173

Romantic games/readings,
178–180

Romany Method, 2, 3, 94–109

Clubs, 95–97

combinations of, 104–107

Diamonds, 97–99

Hearts, 101–104

overview, 94–95

Spades, 99–101

suits, 95

various combinations/inter-
pretations, 108–109

Romany spreads, 110–123

French method, 113–118

Italian method, 118–123

Past, Present and Future
Spread, 110–113

Sevens, 57–61

of Clubs, 58, 97, 129, 160

combinations of, 107

of Diamonds, 59, 99, 127,
160

of Hearts, 61, 103–104, 126,
160

in Master Method, 160

of Spades, 60, 101, 129, 160

symbolism overview, 57

Shuffling, 168

Significator selection, 167–168

Single card, 170

Sixes, 52–56

of Clubs, 53, 131, 160

of Diamonds, 54, 125, 160

of Hearts, 56, 127–128, 160

in Master Method, 160

of Spades, 55, 128, 160

symbolism overview, 52

Spades, 22

Ace, 30, 99, 130, 157

3 (Three), 40

4 (Four), 45

5 (Five), 50

6 (Six), 55, 128, 160

7 (Seven), 60, 101, 129, 160

8 (Eight), 65, 101, 128, 159

9 (Nine), 71, 100–101, 131,
159

10 (Ten), 76, 100, 125, 159

of Hearts, 157

Jack, 81, 100, 127, 158

King, 91, 99–100, 130, 157

Master Method meanings,

142–156
Queen, 86, 100, 126, 158
Romany Method meanings,
    99–101
Twos, 35
Spiritualization of cards, 6–7
Spreads. *See* Lenormand
    spreads; Poker deck spreads;
    Romany spreads; *specific*
    spreads
Square of Thirty-Six. *See*
    Master Method
Suits. *See also specific suits*
    origin of, 15–18
    in Romany Method, 95
    Tarot and, 8, 15–16
Tarot, 1–2, 8, 15–16
Tens, 73–77
    of Clubs, 74, 96, 127, 158
    combinations of, 106
    of Diamonds, 75, 98, 129,
        159
    of Hearts, 77, 102–103, 128,
        159

in Master Method, 158–159
    of Spades, 76, 100, 125, 159
    symbolism overview, 73
This book, using, 2–3
Three-Card Spread, 170–171
Threes, 37–41
    of Clubs, 38
    of Diamonds, 39
    of Hearts, 41
    of Spades, 40
    symbolism overview, 37
Time pattern, 4–5
Twos, 32–36
    of Clubs, 33
    of Diamonds, 34
    of Hearts, 36
    of Spades, 35
    symbolism overview, 32
Values, of cards, 22
Zodiac signs, 15–16, 17–18
    card relationships. *See spe-*
        cific card names
    court card associations, 78